Welfare Titans

and other essays on welfare reform

Welfare Titans:
How Lloyd George and
Gordon Brown Compare

and other essays on welfare reform

Frank Field

Civitas: Institute for the Study of Civil Society
London

First published June 2002

© The Institute for the Study of Civil Society 2002
The Mezzanine, Elizabeth House
39 York Road, London SE1 7NQ
email: books@civitas.org.uk

ISBN 1-903 386-20 9

Typeset by Civitas
in New Century Schoolbook

Printed in Great Britain by
St Edmundsbury Press
Bury St Edmunds, Suffolk

To Michael Anthony Bourke

1958 - 2001

Contents

Author

Frank Field has been Member of Parliament for Birkenhead since 1979 and was Minister for Welfare Reform from the election in 1997 until his resignation 14 months later.

He was the director of the Child Poverty Action Group from 1969 - 1979 and of the Low Pay Unit from 1974 - 1980. He is the author of a number of publications on low pay, poverty and social issues, including *Making Welfare Work* (1995), *How To Pay for the Future* (1996), *Stakeholder Welfare* (1996), *Reforming Welfare* (1997), *The State of Dependency: Welfare Under Labour* (2000), and *Making Welfare Work: Reconstructing Welfare for the Millennium* (2001). He is chair of the Pension Reform Group, of which the first report, *Universal Pensions: Modernising Pensions for the Millennium*, was published in 2001.

Foreword

Reforming welfare has become the Holy Grail of modern political life. Firstly, because cradle-to-grave, rights-based state welfare systems are ruinously expensive. Secondly, because they create dependency on a massive scale. Political parties of different persuasions are struggling, across the Western world, to control the welfare monster which is causing serious damage to our economies and reducing whole swathes of the population to what Frank Field describes as 'a form of permanent serfdom' (p. 59).

In the UK, however, 'ending welfare as we know it' has become one of those meaningless clichés of political life, like 'getting tough on crime'. Both major parties promise it, neither seems capable of delivering it. In fact, as Frank Field argues in this collection of essays, we are moving in exactly the wrong direction. Everything is set to get worse.

Frank Field is a man who knows what he is talking about. He has a lifelong interest in the operation of the welfare system. He has studied it and thought about it. He has worked with constituents who experience its drawbacks first-hand. This has made him realistic about what can be achieved, and convinced him that systems must work with the grain of human nature, or they will fail (p. 22, 25-6)

Unusually, Frank Field is a member of parliament who has a strong sense of history. He talks about current problems in the context of what Beatrice and Sidney Webb believed, what Helen Bosanquet wrote, what the Royal Commission on the Poor Laws recommended in 1909, and how friendly societies operated in the nineteenth century. Rightly or wrongly, Tony Blair's government is thought to have little interest in history. (The contents of the ill-fated Millennium Dome certainly provided ammunition for this particular line of attack.) In the field of welfare policy, this is particularly dangerous, since—as the old adage goes—those who are ignorant of history are doomed to repeat its mistakes, and the mistakes in this particular area are potentially devastating. In one of the most memorable phrases in this book, Frank Field accuses the working families tax credit—the showpiece of New Labour's welfare policy—of ripping out the mainspring of a free society, which is 'the drive to improve one's own lot and that of one's family'. As he says, this 'cannot but harbinger ill for our country' (p. 60).

Which brings us to another important point about Frank Field: he writes extremely well. Accustomed as we are to spin, prevarication, blandness, chronological inexactitudes and misleading the House, it comes as a surprise to find a politician who writes in an elegant and forceful style, making a coherent case and appealing to the good sense and goodwill of the reader.

Frank Field leaves us in no doubt about the seriousness of the situation. The hour of the 'ration-book' approach to welfare, with the state distributing benefits from a common pot to supplicant and docile citizens, has long past. It suited the post-war years when the legislation which has given us the present welfare state was being passed, but the world has moved on. Unfortunately, New Labour has not moved with it. Still clinging to the ration-book model, unwilling to learn from other countries at a similar stage of economic development, New Labour's welfare strategy is described as 'the last throw in the politics of central control' (p. 41).

In Field's view, the idea that the government can go on raising taxation to pay for an increasingly unresponsive welfare system is unrealistic. Voters will not put up with it, whatever they may be telling opinion polls. Frank Field has much to say in this book about the NHS in particular, which he describes as the 'political live-rail' of the British system (p. 3). There is widespread dissatisfaction with it, but politicians interfere with it at their peril. It is, he says 'the only part of the post-war settlement about which voters care' (p. 3). Nevertheless, Field points out the folly of the present policy of steadfastly refusing to countenance any other method of healthcare provision than a centrally funded, state-controlled system:

> If a one-third real increase in monies going to the NHS does not begin to produce a noticeable improvement in services, for example, what will? That the Secretary of State for Health has to issue a central edict on how to clean hospitals suggests there is a paralys-

ing weakness inherent in a centrally-run service which almost no amount of money will cure (p. 41).

Whilst this book was being prepared for the press Gordon Brown delivered his 2002 budget, which allocated an unprecedented increase in funding for the NHS, without any of the internal reforms which Field and many others, from all sides of the political spectrum, have been calling for. The Prime Minister has acknowledged that if the strategy fails to deliver significant improvements by the next election, voters will judge the government accordingly. This is an unnecessarily high-risk strategy.

Perhaps the most compelling essay in this collection is the one which gives its title to the book. The comparison between Lloyd George and Gordon Brown as reforming Chancellors of the Exchequer is one which only Frank Field could have made. It draws on both his historical research and his practical experience of how welfare systems work.

Both Chancellors have wanted to help the poor, but their methods have reflected radically different views of human nature, and of the proper role of government. Both have seen the need to raise the incomes of the poor, but for Lloyd George this was only part of the problem. He wanted to raise incomes *and* set working men free as independent citizens, capable of improving their lot by their own efforts. The effect of Gordon Brown's reforms, on the other hand, has been to create 'a degree and intensity of dependency for the working population hitherto unknown' (p. 61). Lloyd George constructed a floor on which working people could build. Gordon Brown has constructed a ceiling which is so thick, many will never be able to break through it.

Frank Field speaks on welfare reform with an authority that is unmatched in the Palace of Westminster, and Civitas is proud to publish his latest contribution to one of the most important debates now taking place in the field of public policy. If we fail to find our way out of the present welfare mess, the prospects for a free and prosperous society are bleak. With Frank Field as our guide, we at least have a chance.

Robert Whelan

Acknowledgments

Jill Hendey kindly put in all the work necessary to prepare the initial lectures and the final manuscript for the press. Ben Forsyth worked on the text improving the clarity and presentation of the ideas and arguments. I remain very grateful to both of them.

Mick Bourke chose me as the minister he would drive after the 1997 election. He became a friend and colleague and died with a bravery and quiet dignity I knew he would show at the last. This volume is dedicated to his memory.

Frank Field
5 May 2002

1

Introduction: Taxpayers Awake

This is the parliament for delivery. That was Tony Blair's pledge in response to his second runaway election win. It will also be a parliament where tax and spend raises its ugly head once again. Labour won in 1997 because of Tony Blair's leadership and because it pledged not to raise income tax. The nightmare scenario for Labour is for little improvement in public services, or little which registers with the voters, accompanied by increases in direct taxes.

These essays set out themes which are coming alive in this parliament. Labour's first review of public expenditure set record increases in most departmental budgets up to 2003. These increases were way in excess of the growth in the economy and of tax revenues. The projection from 2003 or thereabouts on public expenditure make clear that the budget surplus would be spent and that it would fall to the budget in 2002 to begin setting in place a tax strategy to deal with the growing deficit. At this stage politics would wake from the slumber into which it had fallen in 1997. And so it has proved.

Health has already swooped up the national agenda as a priority issue on which the electorate expects the government to deliver real improvements. At the same time the Blair government is open to regional public service delivery targets. In London, for example, the tube is slowly but surely disintegrating. The most recent sign of this trend is the closing of some central London tube stations during rush hour due to a demand which is too great to meet within acceptable safety rules. Commuters coming into London similarly are increasingly being required to pay top prices for a third world service.

In a significant number of areas of the country there are now fewer people in work than at the 1997 election. While

1.25 million additional jobs have been created during this time their distribution has been uneven. 252 MPs now represent seats where the employment rate is lower than when Labour first won power. New Deal's £4 bn expenditure fails to redress this balance.

The size of the welfare budget is set also to reappear, rather as Banquo's Ghost, at Labour's next election banquet. In 1997 the party was elected on a clear mandate to cut welfare expenditure—welfare bills, the electorate were told, rose as a direct result of Tory failure. Health and education budgets were to be boosted by transferring funds from a sharply reined-back welfare budget. Leaving direct taxes to finance the public services revolution was not an option. Yet despite unemployment being reduced to around a million, the welfare bills are now rising swiftly.

Under the five years of the Major government, welfare expenditure grew by eleven per cent in real terms. Taking 1997-8 as the base, welfare bills including the working families tax credit and the disabled person's tax credit have risen from £102.6 bn to £112.8 bn—an increase of 10 per cent by 2001-02. If the projection is taken a couple of years on to 2003-04, thereby including the costs of the initial stages of the pension credit, the welfare bill rises to a minimum of £122 bn, giving an increase of nine per cent in welfare expenditure in real terms. So much for Tory failure.

But it will be in the NHS that the politics will be most keenly felt and where they will become pivotal to the life of the government on two fronts. The first front centres on raising direct taxes while the second focuses on reforming the NHS from a producer-dominated to a consumer-led operation. Can Britain's last nationalised industry be reformed fast enough to keep up with the consumer revolution now trying to push its way through public services? And can a new tax contract be successfully negotiated with voters to meet a rising NHS bill?

The electoral barriers to Labour entering Downing Street were only dismantled by the pledge Labour gave in 1997 that it was a low-tax party. That taxes would have to rise in this parliament, or the level of finance for public services be cut, was one of the central debates before the 2001 General Election. In the post-1997 world, raising direct taxes opens up a new political ball game.

The tax debate has moved on since the 2001 election, although it is important to remember what the issue was at the polls. At the polls voters did have a choice, although most politicians have continued to mistake what that choice was. The Tories emphasised tax cuts while Labour stressed its priority to increasing public expenditure. The Tories did not lose the election because of their tax strategy. They lost in 2001 despite their promise on tax. Voters were not prepared at that stage to forgive them for their past misdeeds.

It is here that the NHS comes into full play. In Europe electorates are prepared to kill governments which tamper with public pension provision. In Britain the equivalent political live-rail is health. The NHS is now, and always was perhaps, the only part of the post-war settlement about which voters care. Politicians attempt to reform the NHS at their peril, and this remains true even when the demand for reform comes from the voters themselves.

Pollsters have long reported a willingness amongst voters to see income tax rise, and the strategy Gordon Brown is pursuing in his 2002 budget will test the truthfulness of voters to the limit. I have never accepted these findings at face value. Appearing high-minded to the pollster is a game voters are prepared to play when they know that no party interested in getting elected will mistake rhetoric for reality. Voters are older, wiser and generally richer than they were when they last faced a government contemplating income tax increases. Labour misreads the last election result if it believes it has a groundswell of support for general direct tax increases.

Voters are rightly cynical as to what else the government might try and raise money for, using the cry of more funds for the NHS as its cover. If the NHS is going to have more money over the longer term taxpayers will demand in return a new tax contract. The form this tax contract will take is another theme examined in these essays. The age of unhypothecated direct tax increases is over. From now on voters may sanction tax rises, but any increases will have to be covenanted to targeted changes in the NHS, and perhaps one or two other key services such as the numbers of police on the beat. Moreover taxpayers will want first to see that their existing tax payments are bringing about improvements in services before meeting higher tax bills out of their income.

A further theme of these essays is that the continuance of universal services is dependent on a growing provision from outside the state sector. The idea that an adequate health service can be delivered by the old ration-book type of approach would be laughable if there were not so many politically invested interests wedded to this belief. The biggest ever increase in taxpayers' largesse—a cool £12 bn—has already been allocated without any significant visible change at all in the NHS's performance, and there is much more planned from the same source.

The outline of an alternative NHS reform programme is given here. Crucial to this genuine third way is to hand back the NHS to local communities who controlled the service prior to nationalisation in 1948. The alternative to a locally directed collective service is a further and possible fatal weakening of the NHS as richer, and sometimes not so rich, taxpayers desert.

Chapter 4 contrasts Gordon Brown with Lloyd George as welfare reformers. The fundamental difference between these two major figures as Chancellors of the Exchequer derives from what they see as the goal of welfare reform. Gordon Brown has an essentially one-dimensional view where the object of his tax credit strategy is to increase the income of the poor. This is no mean objective.

Its limitations, however, become quickly apparent as soon as Lloyd George's dual objectives in welfare reform are considered. Lloyd George shared Gordon Brown's objective of channelling more money to the poor. But of equal importance to Lloyd George was the objective of combining increases of income for the poor with extending their freedom.

Gordon Brown's strategy achieves the opposite. Indeed, in a cruel paradox, the more money that goes to the poor by way of means-testing, the greater is the restriction on their freedom. Tax credits make it impossible for a growing army of individuals to improve their family's income and well-being by working harder or longer or gaining additional qualifications.

All such efforts are penalised by the withdrawal of tax credits. One tax credit recipient reported in a television news broadcast his pleasure at receiving tax credit help, but then ominously added that he realised from now on he would never ever be able to improve his family's income and well-being by his own efforts. He was now totally dependent on decisions politicians make for that to occur. The Institute for Fiscal Studies estimates that 83 per cent of families with children will be eligible for the working families tax credit. And in its latest reform the government will extend the tax credit to workers without children. No free society can function when very large sections of the working population are so imprisoned in a welfare system that their own efforts can make little difference to their income.

Tax credits will follow the trajectory pioneered by housing benefit. At first, few people spoke against a scheme which ostensibly helped the poor to pay their rent. Warnings that housing benefit would push up rents to a level which increasingly working people would not be able to afford, and that fraud would be endemic in the system, were dismissed as irrelevancies.

Similarly, warnings that tax credits will push modest wage levels down towards the minimum wage level, not surprisingly, remain unheeded. For a growing body of employers, together with a growing army of workers, any reasonable wage increase cannot break through the take-home pay which low wages and high tax credits provide. Fraud will follow the pattern set out by family credit, the precursor of the tax credit strategy. Employers and workers then came to agreements that formal wage levels would be recorded at the level at which maximum family credit payments could be made, with many employers paying supplements in cash to working people willing to collude in fraud at the expense of taxpayers.

While few people spoke against the introduction of housing benefit, even fewer people now defend its existence. But with rents pushed up to record levels and 3.8 million households claiming benefit, politicians are at a loss how to jump off this welfare treadmill. At some stage soon the tax credit reforms will follow this pattern. The cost is already very considerable, amounting to 3p on the standard rate of tax, and the bill is rising. Once the other tax credits are added in the sum becomes the equivalent to what a 4p cut in the standard rate of tax would cost to implement.

As with housing benefit, there is no easy way of disengaging from the tax credit labyrinth. A simple abolition is not on the cards. Too many families gain too much of their total income from tax credits for that to be a fair or wise reform strategy. Seventy thousand families, for example, have their original incomes at least doubled by the working families tax credit.

There is, however, an exit strategy. An incoming government could promise to freeze the value of all tax credit payments. As part of this strategy it should also pledge itself to offer tax cuts to the value of the revenue which would otherwise have been devoted in each annual uprating of the credits.

Offering this alternative to what must otherwise be a growing tax credit budget could have considerable electoral appeal. If pensioners had been offered a £10 a week rise in their retirement pension for pensioners over 75, how many would have voted for having a pensioner tax credit? Not many, I think. A similar appeal could be made, I believe, to lower-paid workers. A reduction of the standard rate of tax to 18p in the pound would, I believe, have had a large number of backers from the tax credit rolls as well as from the electoral roll.

Tax credits are the Chancellor's personal welfare reform strategy. The success of this approach is measured only by the numbers claiming help, and such is the effort to get individuals to claim entitlement that any policing of taxpayers' money has been downgraded to the point where its existence is noticeable only by its absence. That welfare reform has to be built so that it works with the grain of human nature—of directing self-interest so that it promotes work, savings and honesty—is a lesson which I thought had been learnt before Labour's 1997 election win. That lesson will have to be learnt again, but this time in the wake of a collapsing tax credit system.

2

Welfare Reform and Citizenship: Devaluing the Poor

Summary

*W**elfare reform, if it is to be successful in the longer-term, needs to be based on a carefully thought out political strategy. The new political arithmetic, where the poor are an electoral minority, and many working-class voters have rising aspirations, requires welfare reform to appeal to the interests of the majority. While welfare reform similarly must work with rather than against the grain of human nature, self-interest has to be harnessed in a way which builds an inclusive programme. The government's drive towards ever greater means-tested provision looks good in year one. The penalties means-tests impose on working, saving and honesty become apparent only later with an ever-growing proportion of the population having to think about how best to work this system. Equally importantly, this drive to even greater means-tested dependency is set to blow apart some of the key characteristics which underpin a common citizenship.*

Introduction

Winston Churchill, as a junior member of the Liberal government, turned his mind in 1908 to the question of how best to mitigate the evil influences of unemployment on families. He referred to this issue as that 'untrodden field of politics'.[1] So too with the idea of citizenship in the English political tradition. The word citizenship is rarely given any

---

Given as a Stevenson Lecture in Citizenship at the University of Glasgow, 18 April 2000.

9

clear meaning in political ideas or political activity. It is nevertheless of considerable political significance.

Welfare reform needs not only to be thought out carefully, but it has also to be backed by a coherent and inclusive political strategy if it is to be successful. Indeed, the importance of this political strategy is such that it must help shape how principles may be translated into working reforms. The expectation (certainly my expectation) was that thinking the unthinkable would form the basis of the welfare reform strategy Labour would advance in office. To illustrate the politics of welfare reform I shall endeavour to introduce you to how stakeholder pensions could have been constituted. By turning its back on this approach, the government has been forced to concede a growing dominance to means-tested welfare, with devastating consequences for citizenship in the twenty-first century.

Not By the Poor Alone

A new political arithmetic of our age was the starting point underpinning the politics of thinking the unthinkable. Expressed crudely, there have already been three periods with their own distinct political arithmetic in modern politics. There was, first, that which operated before the advent of the universal franchise, which is itself a fairly recent phenomenon in Britain, although we sometimes convince ourselves otherwise.[2]

During this first stage political leaders, such as Peel and Gladstone, were adamant that parties should not produce programmes until they were 'called in' as it was known. The phrase, presumably, derived from the monarch summonsing, or calling to the Palace, a political leader and inviting them to form an administration. The rhetoric was nothing if not proud. Politicians were there to exercise judgement and not to be swayed by the preferences of voters. Given that this was still an age when landed magnates could and did determine not only the choice of some candidates, but which of those candidates were successful, the 'no policy' declaration until a leader was 'called in' did not fully describe the subtlety of the political process. Here, then,

was a political arithmetic where interests were represented
in Parliament but in a manner totally foreign to our current
democratic comprehension.[3]

It is not hard to imagine the shock when someone who
had *made* their fortune, rather than inherited it, and done
so from *trade*, rather than from land, challenged this
thinking and heralded the 'age of ransom'. In this short,
tough, explosive phrase, Joseph Chamberlain delivered an
unyielding message. If the rich wanted to keep most of their
loot they would have to buy off poorer voters with social
reform. Here, then, was the second era of political arithmetic. Politicians of all parties sought an election victory on
the basis of offering gains for the working class paid for
with money taken from other voters.

The age of the 'have-nots' comprising a majority of the
electorate spilled over into quite recent times. To be a
majority group does not, of course, mean that the majority
voted as a single entity. The party of the left had to appear
a credible government for that to happen. Yet, looking again
recently at the Socialist Commentary's *Must Labour Lose?*[4]
report, I was struck by just how large a proportion of
Labour voters in the 1960s saw the party they supported as
championing the under-dog, factory workers, pensioners
and poor people.

The politics of ransom provided a political cover for the
poor. We are still talking of a time when there was a large
overlap between being working-class and being poor. There
were marked differences, of course, between those at the top
and at the bottom end of the working-class income spectrum. But there was enough common ground still to make
an electoral appeal relevant to poor and non-poor working
class alike.

Protecting and promoting the interest of the poor today
takes us into political arithmetic's third age. For the first
time a sizeable part of the working class and lower middle
class now have incomes which give them real choices. They
rarely look to those below them. They associate themselves
increasingly with the aspirations common amongst those
higher up the social hierarchy. Gaining reforms paid for by

someone else's money is one matter. Being expected to pay for your own reforms puts the issue into a different focus. Moreover, paying for the reforms over which you have little say is guaranteed to generate friction. This third age is therefore one where consumer interests replace the dominance of producer or class interests.

A ration-book fare from central government has less and less appeal for these new discerning consumers. Choices can and are made. Look, for example, at how the holiday trade has been transformed. It was not that long ago when the so-called enlightened middle classes scoffed at the idea of working-class people holidaying abroad. Similarly, the left, in particular, has been loath to enfranchise public sector consumers. Yet, within the severe restraints imposed upon them, many voters are trying to insist on choice in what remains of the public sector.

In the third age of political arithmetic the traditional approach to social reform no longer commands enough support to win elections. Rousing calls of fraternal greetings, of common endeavours and the like, are important for the political platform, although, even here, the audience has for the most part quietly tip-toed away. Altruism alone is not strong enough or durable enough to sustain a radical programme. An appeal to the self-interest of the majority has to be clearly pitched, and it is only within this appeal that the interests of the poor can now be advanced.

Self-interest and the Common Good

The role of self-interest raises a second strand of the politics of thinking the unthinkable. Self interest is basic and intrinsic to human nature. How otherwise would mankind ever survive? But while self-interest is distinct from selfishness, and selfishness is a different stimulus from greed, self-interest does not automatically, or even necessarily, preclude altruistic intent. In the post-Freudian age we perhaps ought to know better than to assert a purity of motive for any single action or thought. I would guess that altruism is very often underpinned by self-interest. (It certainly is in the USA where it is tax deductible!) That is not in any way to devalue altruistic intent. It certainly does not lessen its effect. It is merely to draw attention to a force strengthening its durability.

The new political arithmetic demands that if policies are to have a chance of being carried at the election they must have a majority appeal. But it is possible to make such a pitch, and make the approach comprehensive in order to include the poor. Of course, a majority appeal does not automatically ensure comprehensiveness. But these two goals are not inevitably opposed.

To illustrate the other assumptions which underpinned the political strategy of thinking the unthinkable, I wish to concentrate on pensions reform. It would be possible to recast the stakeholder pension from its present mould shaped by the personal pension régime and to build it as a guarantee, offering a pension valued at a set level of average earnings. Such a scheme would see the achievement of a number of aspects of thinking the unthinkable.

It would establish a link between self-interest and the welfare of the poorest. A pension guarantee set as a percentage of average earnings cannot be bought in the private market other than by the seriously rich, and they, not surprisingly, are unlikely to be interested in a stakeholder guarantee. Such a guarantee can only be offered to ordinary voters if it is underwritten by the community as a whole.

Universal But Not State

This form of stakeholder pension illustrates how universal coverage can be gained in an era of non-government provision. Indeed, looking beyond government may be the *only* means by which a new universalism can be established in respect of pensions which is, after all, by far and away the largest item of expenditure in the traditional welfare budget.

The proposal I put forward in government was for new recruits to the labour market to be required to contribute to a funded pension as well as their national insurance pension. The aim of both contributions would be to accumulate funds sufficient to offer a stakeholder pension set at a high enough proportion of average earnings to ensure that all pensioners were lifted free of means-tested entitlement.

The funded side of the scheme would not be divided up into little personal pots of wealth, as is the norm for personal pensions, but kept as part of a number of large investment funds. Compulsion is crucial to the success of this proposal. All those in employment above a very low income threshold would have to be in a stakeholder pension scheme. But, because of the attractiveness of the idea—it cannot be bought elsewhere—self-interest could allow some form of graduated contributions: i.e. self-interest could support the altruistic objective of raising the funds within the scheme to include the poor.[5]

Sending the Right Message

This is not the place for the full details of this proposal, but one important advantage of such an approach is that it would send out all the right messages on work and saving. This is in stark contrast to the messages emanating from the government's means-tested minimum income guarantee. This means-tested approach results in possibly 40 per cent of the working population being unable to save enough to provide an income greater than that which comes from the minimum income guarantee. Saving has become worse than a useless activity. It is positively dangerous to the financial health of a very significant proportion of the population. And this is not simply a debating point. The government's short-term minimum income guarantee reform undermines the sense of saving for the long term. Already there is evidence showing retired lower-paid workers with small occupational pensions finding themselves worse off than neighbours who refused membership, and also those who had the money but who refused to save, preferring to spend today and let taxpayers look after them tomorrow. What message does this send to the next generation of potential savers? In an attempt to abate the impact of means-tested help, whereby some pensioners who have saved are worse off than those who have not, the government plans to introduce another means test—the pension credit. The impact of the credit will be to shift up the income scale the group who lose out as means-tested help is withdrawn.

A universal stakeholder pension can guarantee that all those on low incomes will keep all the savings they have made in addition to their contributions towards a stakeholder scheme. None will be clawed back through any means-test. It also sends out the right message to those who cannot work at any one time. Providing people in this category fulfil the conditions as a carer or, as unemployed people, are actively seeking work, their contributions will be paid each year to the stakeholder pension plan. This group of the population would therefore know that when they are able to work again they would be building upon an accumulating pension entitlement, and not be faced with the prospect of perhaps being too old to join a pension scheme.

Transparent Redistribution

This single pension reform illustrates three other aspects of the political strategy aimed at fundamental welfare reform. First, the age when taxpayers are prepared to finance significant unconditional redistribution is passing. This is not to say that redistribution is impossible. It is, however, a plea to stand conventional wisdom on its head. Rather than the redistribution being hidden from the electorate as the only way of achieving this end, it needs to be made transparent. If this redistribution is to be sustained over the longer term it also needs to be linked to encouraging behaviour that taxpayers believe enhances the public good.

The pension scheme I have described sets out to meet these objectives. The extent of redistribution is there for everyone to see. Indeed, it might be said that the scheme errs on the side of rubbing the noses of contributors into this very fact. This transparency is, I believe, crucial. The standing of politicians is low. Political activity is mocked, if not despised. To try and hoodwink voters on this, or any other major issue, might work for a while, but it courts a nasty backlash when voters rumble, as they surely will, what the hidden agenda is.

Best Form of Contract

Next, the scheme also builds on the belief that, while no arrangement can be expected to last into the very long term, history points to some contracts having a longer life expectancy than others. In welfare there are two ways of financing a pensions programme. Both make claims on any year's national income. The first attempts to bind taxpayers into transferring income. The second is to build up holdings of capital, and for this capital ownership to be used as a means of lodging a claim on any year's national income. And both approaches are necessary, I believe, in any sensible welfare settlement. But, on the question of extending welfare provision, for that is what pension reform is fundamentally about, I believe the balance of argument is in favour of greater funded provision. History teaches that, in this country at least, claims on national income by way of dividend payments are met more easily than taxpayers finding themselves committed by previous generations to a high level of taxation.[6]

But funding is not the panacea that it is often thought to be. Indeed, the one which holds the better track record for delivering payments, via wealth-holdings, could be overturned if a future generation feels that the wealth-holders have an unfair claim on national income. The overturning may come by political means, i.e. through the ballot box. Or the challenge could be economic, whereby workers push up inflation to cut the real income levels of wealth-holders.

A third political judgement centres on what the best arrangements might be for spreading risks common to practically the whole community. Here the debate is usually crudely polarised, with collective provision being pitched against market arrangements. But collective provision here does not mean state provision, and collective provision can be such as to draw upon a market spirit in its administration.

Collective Non-state Provision

From the perspective of the years just prior to the outbreak of the First World War, most observers would have predicted that Britain's welfare would continue to develop along the highly decentralised lines of membership-owned organisations.[7] This is not the place to discuss why, 50 years later, this country had one of the most highly centralised and government-run welfare states in the free world. What is important is to register that the 'coming of the welfare state', as so many text books bill these events, was neither inevitable in this form, nor did it mark the utopian end-game as far as welfare was concerned.

Collective provision is still the best way to advance in covering common risks. With risks spread over the greatest number of people, average costs are low. As cherry picking is not allowed, taxpayers are not left to underwrite the costs of those with the greatest risks whom the market refuses to cover. But collective provision is not necessarily synonymous with a state-run system. Here was another key political judgement. Welfare expenditure needs to increase—many more of us are, for example, living longer, and pensions therefore need to be drawn over a longer time span. Yet individuals generally are resistant to increased taxation, and increased state provision, as a means of delivering this expanded welfare package.

The increasing cost of welfare might be borne collectively, and therefore cover the poor, if new membership-based organisations were established to control and handle the assets, and to distribute the benefits. In other words, by putting government, as we currently know it, at arm's length. By achieving this goal—and so allowing comprehensiveness—another equally important goal is achieved. Welfare reform dovetails with the more traditional constitutional reform debate. But in place of devolving power to geographical regions, this programme of reform is about extending the power of individuals within new membership-owned organisations. Increasing individual control over welfare assets is, I believe, the *quid pro quo* of an agreement to save more for a better pension income in the future.

A major task is completed. I have outlined the politics which underpin the welfare strategy I hope the government in the not too distant future will implement. But there is one part of the story which has yet to be told. The government's rhetoric about welfare is markedly different from the line pursued in opposition. Are we in a new era? Or is the old welfare wine merely being put into new bottles? And does the course of reform now being pursued strengthen or destroy one of the major supports for a common citizenship?

New Labour or Old Policies?

Let us go back to the Labour Opposition's central attack on the Tories' welfare budget. While there was a sense of shock when the leadership realised that by far and away the largest part of the government's budget—a cool third—went on welfare, the rate at which this budget was growing, and the negative impact of means-tested welfare on behaviour, also became matters of major political concern.

Indeed, the attack on means-testing was linked to the growth in the budget. By far and away the fastest growing part of the welfare programme was the means-tested element. That proportion of the budget stood at 35 per cent in 1997, up from 13 per cent in 1979. The number of people living in households with at least one member dependent on means-testing had doubled during this time, from one in six to one in three.

The Labour Opposition Front Bench rounded on a government forcing an ever-growing army of pensioners on to means-tested income support. Family credit—a subsidy to low wage-earners—was condemned in similar fashion. It sustained the evil of low wages, it benefited scrooge employers and, by subsidising their wage bill, it not only created unfair competition but distorted the market by its downward push on low wage rates.

The government claims it has halved the growth in the overall welfare budget.[8] Two reasons principally account for this trend. The buoyant economy has played a positive role. In many areas of the country, but alas not all, the increase in the number of jobs has ensured that there is work for people anxious to move off welfare. A series of Tory welfare cuts—hotly opposed by the Labour Opposition—are now in place and having a downward push on the size of the welfare bill. People's entitlements to some benefits have been cut or abolished.

The government's welcome welfare to work strategy is also a factor in the equation. But its importance in reducing unnecessary welfare expenditure is not comparable to these other two factors. Indeed, its costs, so far, outweigh its benefits in terms of reduced welfare expenditure. The programme's impact will however be felt in the longer term. Welfare to work signals a change from what might best be called a passive welfare system, with an operation largely concerned with paying out benefits, to a pro-active one which weighs the crucial task of paying benefit with an equal concern with helping people into work when that is a realistic possibility. The change in public culture these series of welfare to work measures will bring about should not be under-rated. But they are not, as yet, a major influence in the fall in the rate of growth of welfare expenditure.

Behind the bravado claims of welfare success—the 'cuts' in what the budget was forecast to be, falling numbers of young unemployed, the numbers generally moving from benefit to work—lurks the acceptance of an ever-growing role for means-tested welfare. Sooner or later this development will derail the welfare reform strategy on which the government has now embarked.

Means-Tested Welfare

The strategy's presentation is nothing if not ambitious. Just as redistribution has fallen out of the political vocabulary, to be replaced by the concept of fairness, the terms minimum income guarantee and tax credits are used as dazzling headlights. But these headlights are mounted on to the front of a means-tested bandwagon. And no amount of inventiveness over names will prevent the huge downside any means-tested strategy drags in its wake. The attack on work, savings and honesty is inevitable, and the more ambitious the strategy, the greater the destruction on these fronts which will be wrought.

The government's pension strategy already illustrates how short-term means-tested expedience can undermine noble long-term objectives. So as to provide more generous pensions in the future, the government's longer-term strategy is to reverse the current 60-40 rate of publicly financed pensions to private pension provision. A second overall objective is to reduce the number of pensioners on means-tests. If everything goes as planned, the government's long-term reform will see the proportion of pensioners dependent on means-tests falling from one in three to one in four of the pensioner population 50 years hence. And this modest, but not unimportant, reduction assumes the extent of means-tested help to current pensioners will have no adverse long-term effect on savings.

To make this assumption, however, is to stretch realism beyond the bounds of possibility. Buying the new stakeholder pension will be voluntary. Rebates will encourage target workers to join, but there will be no compulsion. And, as I have already noted, at the same time the means-tested minimum income guarantee is currently offering a growing proportion of the population a pension which is more valuable than anything they could acquire by saving. An army of pensioners who did save now would find themselves worse off than if they had simply squandered every penny they had ever had. The dignified but quiet anger expressed by pensioners writing from around the country who feel mocked by a government which rewards those who did not save—I accept there were some who could not have saved — and who rely on future taxpayers to look after them, will not only be registered in a lower turnout at the next election if no action is taken. But within the extended families of these pensioners a most profound questioning is taking place. If working the system is so well rewarded, why not join the crowd?

Extending Means Tests

In his 2000 budget statement, in little more than an aside, Gordon Brown hinted that pensioners would in future be covered by a pensioner credit system. Quite what this involves is only now becoming clearer. What is clear is how extensive is the spread of the tax credit system to those of working age. The flagship in this whole enterprise is the working families tax credit (WFTC) which subsidises low wages and pays a handsome contribution towards childcare. So generous are the proposals that a family with three children may have an income of £40,000 a year and still be claiming WFTC.

But there is a downside to this means-tested approach of making work pay. From net income of £91 and above, families face a withdrawal rate of 55p on the working families tax credit for each £1 rise in earnings. When income tax or national insurance are added in, the tax credit marginal withdrawal rate peaks at 70 per cent, or up to 95 per cent with housing benefit and council tax benefit withdrawal. This is at a time when the 40 per cent marginal tax rate is thought to be the highest that should be levied on top income earners.

Means-testing, it has to be admitted, does encourage entrepreneurial skills. But they are skills associated with working the system and they feed the black market or hidden economy. Means-testing encourages and rewards dishonesty. Family credit, the WFTC's predecessor, invited collusion between employers and employees. Wages were paid at a minimum. Family credit payments came in at a maximum and large sums of cash were drawn on the firm's bank account each week. Employees picked up part of their wages in cash, employers reduced their wage bill at the expense of taxpayers.

The national minimum wage builds a floor below which wages cannot legally be paid. This is an important reform, but between an hourly rate of £3.60 and £5.00, no wage increase can financially improve the worker's take-home pay. As with family credit, the working families tax credit will push low wage rates down towards the national minimum.

We are not talking of a means-tested welfare system affecting a small, declining proportion of the population. The current means-tested strategy will cover 40 per cent of the population, up from a third under the Tories. Once the pensioner credit system is introduced this proportion will surge above the 50 per cent mark.

The lure of the tax credit is powerful. But it is essentially a short-sighted strategy. It offers significant increases in take-home pay. But workers so rewarded find themselves trapped on a welfare treadmill with marginal tax rates of up to 95 per cent slashing any pay increase.

We were told not long ago that you cannot buck the market. Indeed, but the political system bucked the person who told us this truth. Similarly, a welfare reform programme cannot buck human nature. One key aspect of thinking the unthinkable was that welfare had to work with, rather than against, the grain of human nature. Like the bricks made without straw, first appearances tell us nothing about durability. But just as those bricks did not last, disintegrating under the lash of wind and rain, so too a minimum income guarantee, or a tax credit system, cannot survive in the longer-run, no matter how creative the name of the means-tested benefit.

Ricocheting Onto Citizenship

Tax credits are presented as a simple and efficient means of making work pay. They certainly achieve this goal in their first year of operation, but the longer-term impact on a worker's net pay is less straightforward. But tax credits are not simply about modernising the tax and benefit system. They also have the potential to blow apart a major part of the current political agreement on citizenship.

The authority the government claims for its lurch into tax credits is an apparently innocent-sounding sentence in the 1997 manifesto. It reads: 'We will keep under continuous review all aspects of the tax and benefit systems' adding, ironically as matters have turned out, 'to ensure that they are supportive of families and children'.[9] The adequacy of such an oblique authority for a revolution in taxes and benefits may be left unchallenged when the government has a majority of 180 behind it. But this administration has embarked on a high-risk strategy. It is undermining a widely accepted agreement on how people should be treated in some very basic respects, and how to pay for a major part of the government's programme, without discussing, let alone testing, the consequences of such a momentous change. Whether the government realises how profound a change it is attempting to the basis of citizenship in this country is in some doubt.

Just how profound a change is being undertaken is brought into focus if we look at the 1945 settlement which the tax credit system seeks to replace. Not for the first time, Jose Harris plots the subtle movement of debate over the decades which led to the advent of this contract-based citizenship. An insurance-based agreement was established, and remained 'extraordinarily tenacious' because it 'fitted in with the current principles of fiscal reality, and with current evaluations of virtue, citizenship, gender, personal freedom and the nature of the state'.[10]

Destroying the 1945 Settlement

Tax credits strike at each of these foundation props of the 1945 settlement. First, the view about fiscal reality, or people's willingness to pay for a major part of the government's programme. The Chancellor has yet to state that he views insurance contributions as anything but a tax. In the television broadcast following his first budget he referred ominously to the 'national insurance tax'.

What is the sense of regularly referring to a 'national insurance tax' when voters stubbornly refuse to see it as such and insist on it being an insurance contribution? The Tories ruthlessly mined this particular electoral seam. Major increases were also made to national insurance contributions and yet, because cuts were made to the rate of income tax, the Conservatives fought successive elections as a low-tax party, and were believed.

The Chancellor's strategy becomes even more surprising when other attitudes of taxpayers are brought into view. We live in an age when voters will vote against the party seen to be in favour of increasing direct taxes. Steadfastness on this issue in the privacy of the ballot box belies whatever is whispered to pollsters.

In contrast to a marked hostility to raising direct taxation—a hostility which is spreading to indirect taxes—

the voters offer chancellors a hand of friendship on the question of insurance contributions. Such contributions are emphatically not seen as taxes. What sense can be made of the current Chancellor's campaign to equate insurance contributions with taxation? Can such regular 'slips' be put down to carelessness? Or does the Chancellor have a longer-term game-plan which he is loath at present to disclose? Is the aim to abolish the national insurance system?

Foundation Stones of Citizenship

Next, what impact will tax credits have on the gender basis of citizenship? Both Eleanor Rathbone and William Beveridge, along with their campaigners, supported a work-based national insurance system because they saw work in the home as equally valid, and an activity to be rewarded through the insurance system. Our age is still working through a new gender contract, with perhaps much distance still to go. But the threat that tax credits pose to independent taxation, to take one item from the gender contract, is only slowly being recognised. Yet each political concession to re-establishing principles of independent taxation within a tax credit system makes what was allegedly a simple administration of tax credit into one with considerable complications. And one which is more intrusive. Employers have never had to know as much about the private living arrangements of as many of their workforce as they now must know as the administrators responsible for tax credit payments.

How well does today's national insurance system fit with other underpinning views on citizenship—of virtue, freedom and the nature of the state—all of which Jose Harris sees as crucial to the 1945 settlement? Of course the system needs to be modernised. Above all it has to become a scheme where the contributor genuinely feels ownership. But the underlying values of the scheme are, if anything, more relevant now than half a century ago.

The belief that people should look after themselves, if at all possible, remains as strong as ever. Work, savings and honesty, it is believed, should be rewarded and not penalised. Tax credits, the minimum income guarantee, and their like, attack each of these three aspects of the good society. They also attack what is commonly regarded as an important aspect of freedom. A citizen's immediate well-being is enhanced by means-tested help. But an effective counter-poverty strategy is not simply about increasing the poor's immediate income, important as this is. For long-term success it is crucial that the means by which the income of the poor is increased simultaneously widens their freedom. Means tests, because benefits are reduced or withdrawn as income rises, and because savings can disqualify a person from help, place a heavy penalty on telling the truth on either of these two counts. Means tests in the short run increase the poor's income, but only at the great cost of narrowing their freedom.

Conclusion

Let me briefly summarise the points which I have been trying to make. There is a technical side to welfare reform. How are the details of policies worked out? But, of equal importance are the politics of welfare reform. Welfare reform will not be successful if it ignores a number of crucial points on the political compass.

Welfare reform which is beneficial to the poor can only be successfully pursued in the longer run within a framework in which the self-interest of the majority is served.

Universal provision must still be a goal for basic welfare. But in this new political age extending the principle of universalism will only be realisable within a system of joint public-private provision. The phrase private provision should not be simply equated with private company provision. Private provision, i.e. non-state provision, can still be collective provision with welfare provided through membership-owned bodies.

Human nature cannot be written out of the equation. No matter how beguiling a welfare reform programme is, if it works against the grain of human nature, it will in the longer term fail. This will be the fate of the tax credit and minimum income guarantee reforms. The government will soon learn that human nature is not for turning. Worse still, this misadventure blows apart some important sentiments underpinning a common citizenship.

3

New Third Way Politics: a Backward Glance into the Future

Summary

A key part of the current political agenda is the fate of public services. Voters are demanding a radical improvement in the services they pay for through taxation. Labour's strategy of significantly increasing funding, and attaching to these real money increases a growing battery of centrally set targets, will be tested to the full. If the results fail to match rising public expectations, the political initiative will swing to the Right. A strategy to privatise will find the wind once again in its sails. Neither the essentially backward-looking approach of centrally directed public services, nor a questionable privatisation strategy, is likely to deliver what voters want. The demand for commonly owned services, which remains strong, is not matched by public confidence in a centrally directed state service. History teaches us of a genuine third way when education, health and social security flourished beyond the reach of the state. These commonly owned services offer a fruitful insight for third way politics in a second term of Labour government.

Setting the Scene

The social historian Jose Harris, in one of her many perceptive essays, set the scene. One hundred years ago few would have prophesied that by the middle of the twentieth century we would have had one of the most centralised and bureau-

Paper given to Durham University History Society's Annual Conference on 'A Century of Socialism?' 3 February 2001.

cratic of welfare states.[1] At the turn of the twentieth
century Britain's welfare was organised on a totally different basis. Collective welfare existed, but it was organised
largely through member-owned or mutual societies. Above
all, it was locally run, even if organised by national societies. The success which working-class people made of
running these organisations was a key factor in extending
the franchise. If their citizenship had already been proved
by the founding and nurturing of one of the strongest parts
of civil society, on what basis could the vote be denied? Of
course this collective-run non-state welfare had problems,
but none of these pressures would necessarily have prevented an extending of its boundaries to cover an ever
greater proportion of the population.

Events, as we know, turned out very differently. Why the
large institutions making up welfare were shaken like dice
and thrown down to form a very different pattern is not
considered here. An explanation of this unexpected turn of
events—unexpected then, at least—has already been provided. What is surprising is how few people, including
specialists in the field, have any idea of what once was.[2]
Knowledge of life before state welfare might suggest that
the almost universally accepted model of welfare development—the inevitability of charitable, voluntary and mutual
welfare provision giving way to a superior state organised
system—is no more than history being given a particularly
vicious Whiggish spin. More importantly, if state welfare is
not the inevitable end to welfare development, knowledge
of this lost world of welfare could hold out ideas for us on
how welfare might best be reformed during the twenty-first
century.

Why have politicians of the centre-left, and of the right
also, been left in such a state of ignorance as to what once
was in itself a story that would repay closer observation?[3]
Our starting point must be the introductory observation
Geoffrey Finlayson made in his study on the changing
frontiers between state and non-state welfare provision:

> Richard Titmuss wrote that 'when we study welfare systems we see
> that they reflect the dominant cultural and political characteristics
> of their societies'.

More perceptively Finlayson recognised:

> It is also true that *studies* of welfare systems reflect such 'dominant cultural and political characteristics'.[4]

A left-wing hegemony held sway. This was reflected in Titmuss's own thinking which dominated, and still does to some extent, the left-wing interpretation of welfare development. It swept all before it. So strong was the tide that for most of the post-war years the Right accepted this approach with a meekness which speaks volumes about the character of the times through which we have lived.

The armies of the left not only won the battle of ideas. Their pounding of enemy territory was such that few of the old country's contours remained recognisable to those who bothered to look. But this essay is not an attempt to understand how it is that societies wipe clean their collective memories. It is rather to look at three areas of the old homeland and suggest that knowledge of how welfare was organised in education, health and in social security, gives us a guide to what a truly radical agenda could look like today, and that this third way in welfare may offer the best chance there is of maintaining public support for common services.

Education

Few people now realise that perhaps a quarter of all eligible children were once educated in private schools.[5] I am not referring to the kind of schools which now run under this title. What I am talking about are the private schools financed by the penny contributions of poor parents. Prior to the late 1870s, when the determined efforts by Liberal and Tory governments finally defeated parental choice, parents had to pay school attendance fees. And many parents matched the payment of fees with the exercise of choice over the kind of education they wished for their children. Choice in publicly run services is now on the political agenda, although it is being presented as though it is the first time such a concept has existed in Britain. One of the many issues raised by the tale I wish to tell is how imposing a state-run service eliminated parental choice—

except for the very rich who were able to opt out of the state system. Moreover, most people on the left who use the term 'private schools' still do so as a term of abuse. There is little hint in what is said that working-class private schools were often the first choice of poorer parents, and that it was only when radicals had regulated these schools out of existence, and thereby limited the choice open to working-class parents, that the term private school began to be used in a pejorative and élitist way.

The turn of events regarding these schools is rich in irony in other ways as well. It is noticeable that some of the best specialist histories of the period make no mention of them.[6] On the few occasions when this system of working-class run education is recalled, the reference is invariably dismissive.[7] While these schools are stigmatised as dame schools, no feminist to my knowledge has bothered to spend a moment on one of the most interesting of nineteenth century services run almost exclusively by women and legislated out of existence by a parliament totally composed of men.

There is necessarily great difficulty in piecing together an accurate account of the number of such establishments, let alone what precisely they achieved. The records of most of these schools do not now exist. By their very nature, the schools minimised administration. Few of the pupils wrote diaries, and even fewer autobiographies upon which we might now draw. History then, even more than now, was written from the records of the writing class, and from what records those with time, money and space decide to keep. These were schools outside the official system. By today's standards some probably left much to be desired—but then so too do all too many of today's schools. There may also be a question of how successful some of these schools were in educating pupils in what we now see as essential skills, although more thoughtful critics at the time, when looking at the loss of the country's competitive edge against Germany and the United States, posed similar questions about the official state system, as well as the public schools.

What is important to record is the official hostility which these schools generated. When the time came to attack, education officials were given the brief to close them by fair means or foul. One of the ways of assailing them was to insist that schools, in the jargon of the day, had to be inspected to gain a proficiency certificate, and that only proficient schools would be eligible for taxpayers' support. Most of the working-class private schools, like their clients, were deeply suspicious of those public officials whose remit was to check up only on the working class.[8]

Why did it take a whole series of offensives launched by local officials, aided and abetted by local and national politicians, before these schools finally succumbed? The answer is quite simple. These schools were deemed highly popular by the parents who used them.

Indeed the first reason for the existence of the schools is perhaps the most shocking to modern ears used to the theme that the politics of welfare is about doing things to people, rather than enabling people to do their own thing. Faced with the need to educate their children, a very large part of the working class simply set about doing just that, in schools that they set up and paid for themselves.

The schools' popularity followed from this. Their time-tabling met the needs of the parents, again a reason which shocks modern sentiments. With pressures, not to say crises, being all too regular occurrences in working-class households—like all households, in fact, but with far fewer resources to counter them—attending school would sometimes take the strain. And, in taking the strain, the schools responded with sympathy, acting in stark contrast to the state schools whose most likely response would be the issuing of reprimands, or the making of threats.

Wet weather would mean that children forced to attend school at a set time could arrive soaked and remain so all day—or at least until their body heat dried them out. Their self-governed schools understood the sense of not venturing out in the middle of a storm with little clothing anyway, let alone specifically designed protective wear. Discipline also seems to have been an issue. Many working-class parents were not that keen on their children being beaten by middle-class teachers under the guise of good discipline.

All of the three areas cited in this essay—education, social security and health—were treated in the same way by reformers. Reforms were put in place which had the effect of replacing working class-run welfare. Only the method and speed of execution varied.

The first staged execution of educational freedom begins with the 1870 Education Act. Modern eyes understandably view this Act in a favourable light. From it we recognise the system of education we have today. The Act not only brought elementary schooling within the reach of all, but was a clear example of a benevolent state exercising a moral duty on behalf of all its citizens. To the proprietors of the working-class school, and to the parents themselves, the Act appeared in a very different light.

Private schools were not forbidden by the Act. There were too many such schools used by the middle and upper classes for such a direct onslaught to be made. Indeed, the reformers at first thought they would have little to battle against. Once state schools were on offer, their transparent superiority over the private product would be so obvious that the opposition of even the most recalcitrant of parents would collapse. Such parents would simply desert and move over to the superior service. Such simple optimism proved misfounded. Other weapons had to be brought onto the battle field.

The idea of checking the standards of teachers also offered an opening, but was quickly dropped. The fear here was of stirring up public opposition which the hounding of individual teachers would inevitably excite. A more circuitous route had to be taken. Slowly a battle plan was evolved. There was going to be no knockout blow. Instead a whole series of skirmishes were to be mounted, each of them aimed at harassing working-class parents who chose their own school.

Against such actions, parents had little material and no organisational support—a clear difference with today when much of the media would have championed their cause. The Act was presented by officials to parents as outlawing their schools—which it didn't. Surveys were undertaken to find out the spread of schools, but many of those surveyed rightly feared that lists were being compiled so that attacks could be more accurately targeted. Inspection then followed to see if the schools were deemed proficient and thereby eligible to receive the annual grant stipulated by the Act. Local sanitary authorities were joined in the battle. And, at the end of the road, and if necessary, parents might find themselves before the local magistrate for the non-attendance at school of their children.

Despite this array of attacks, the state failed to close working-class private schools on the scale it wished. When the final blow came, not only was it from an unexpected quarter—from the Disraeli government in 1876—but it has all the hallmarks of a strategy upon which the government stumbled. The Vice President of the Council—the education minister—Lord Sandon was described as the mildest mannered man that ever slit a throat![9] And it was from the apparently least obnoxious of measures that he fashioned the stiletto. Not many thrusts were needed to bleed to death working-class support. Children leaving school for work between the ages of 10 and 14 had under the 1876 Act to be in possession of a leaving certificate which related to the level of their abilities or, failing the ability test, to their regular attendance. These certificates could only be issued by a certified proficient school—a status to which most working-class schools were not prepared to seek admittance. No certificate, no job. End of schools. Most of them died quickly and their existence in the public consciousness vanished equally quickly.

Why should it have been otherwise? If a society sees the extension of state provision as morally superior to whatever else had been offered, why bother to record the passing, let alone the extent of support these schools once commanded. But if a near monopoly state provision is simply a stage in history, and not a final destination to which we are all propelled, this story is well worth recalling. And if that state provision fails to live up to expectations, and new ways of providing common services run by the people for the people themselves are genuinely sought, then *The Lost Elementary Schools of Victorian England*, as the title of their study is called, might hold some important lessons for the development of a radical alternative to today's all too obviously unsatisfactory status quo.

Social Security

Welfare is presented differently to education in public ideology. Here the past is not airbrushed out of existence. Rather its existence is admitted, but only in order to present the triumphal progress to state welfare. The thinking here can best be described in allegorical terms, with welfare seen as a train journey. There are stations on the way, appropriately named charitable, voluntary and mutual, but the welfare train has a set destination and one destination only. That terminus is state welfare. Moreover, now that the train has arrived at its final platform, carefully driven by Mr Attlee, no plans are afoot for any further journeys. People wishing to move beyond the terminus are free to make their own arrangements, but no journey by the train offering collective passage is to be provided.

Whether this way of interpreting welfare history is a crude Whiggish or a Marxist interpretation we can safely side-step. What is of importance here is that such a view of welfare, developing inevitably through infant stages to the full mature state welfare, implants a particular squint into the eye of the beholder. All forms of welfare prior to its nationalisation in 1948 are viewed, *ipso facto*, as inadequate, immature or what have you. The way in which these earlier stages are spoken of determines how generations which follow inevitably see these developments of pre-state welfare as being of nothing other than a cursory historical interest. Once again the story contains no lessons, and above all suggests no principles on which welfare ought to be reformed and advanced.

But if state welfare is not seen as an inevitable end to welfare development, then what once existed might usefully be viewed in a very different light. There has been a national system of welfare in Britain for more than five hundred years. What are of particular interest here are the developments in the nineteenth century which centered on the provision of collective welfare outside the state. Indeed, the suppliers and financiers of this collective welfare saw the state in terms of the enemy and, for most of the time, believed that no spoon had a handle long enough to offer their organisation safety while supping with central government. I am of course talking about the extraordinary growth of friendly societies and mutual aid organisations in what is now a hundred or more years ago. In its heyday this movement had a membership six times that of the trade unions. Perhaps even more surprising is that, even after a century of onslaughts by the state, today's membership still outnumbers the affiliated membership to the TUC, a fact which probably tells us more about the perilous state of trade unions than of mutuality's strength.

The mutual aid movement cannot seriously be divorced from those ideas which played such an effective part in shaping the nineteenth century and which helped propel Britain to the top of the economic league table. Here was a movement which had such a view of human nobility that the left-wing line, 'it is the system's fault', played no part in the strategy they devised. Many of the members probably held strong views about how some, and maybe many, of the Victorian capitalists behaved. But there was no room for political philosophy which stated that, until the system was overthrown, nothing could be achieved.

Indeed it was by developing their own strategy that the mutual aid movement did change the world in which they lived. A form of collective social security was devised. Membership of friendly societies became part of a member's life and, in many instances, became one of the most inter-esting parts of it. The responsibility of investing the mem-bership's money, and the building of an administrative machine to check the legitimacy of claims and then to pay benefits, was planned and then manned. For the member-ship, the fear of destitution was pushed that little bit further into the distance. There was a real sense that through these schemes of collective security some control was gained over those elements that could knock away the legs from underneath a working family. We do not have the tools to measure the sense of dignity and worth which derive from such achievements.

These self-governing institutions were the driving force for the social advance which played such a formative role in transforming how skilled working-class people lived in late Victorian Britain. Its success was so marked that reformers from different wings of the political spectrum set about trying to find out how this method could be universalised so as to cover members of unskilled occupations. From this drive to spread success the seeds were sown which would one day grow and choke the parent plant.

One author has described this battle of ideas amongst social reformers as *An Edwardian Mixed Doubles*.[10] The four leading players, but by no means the only ones, were, on the one side, Sidney and Beatrice Webb, and, on the other side, Helen and Bernard Bosanquet. From their study of mutual institutions, the Webbs sought to make the gains universal. The means of spreading this success was not by voluntary effort but by legislation. The Bosanquets—now crudely portrayed in most of those textbooks which bother to mention them—were equally committed to the spread of this welfare success and, equally important, its impact on the development of an active citizenship. They believed, however, that there was something about the mechanism of a voluntary act which helped guarantee the success. They did not believe that this success could be legislated into being by state action. The feeling of ownership resulted in members ensuring that their funds were used properly and fraud countered effectively. There was also a feeling that fraternity went beyond the money benefits of the society. Fraternity was a concept which could only be lived. Hence the personal attention to the care of the sick and of organising what appeared to be an ever growing array of social events.

The outcome of this battle is now history. We know which side won the mixed doubles match. Again, the deed was done by the simplest of measures. At a crucial stage of negotiations over what became the 1911 National Insurance Act—the attempt to universalise the success of mutual aid bodies—Lloyd George made one fatal mistake. He allowed the commercial insurance companies to come within the scheme. The pressure for quick returns and political safety were what decided the issue in Lloyd George's mind. The commercial insurance companies' network offered Lloyd George an immediate and near comprehensive framework through which to run his scheme. These companies, equally significantly, posed a political threat. Their agents called each week at the doors of millions of working-class subscribers. These agents had already shown their muscle in promises they extracted from their customers during the 1910 election. The directors of these companies were generally public backers of the Liberal cause. The man who did so much work in translating the ideas of insurance into a national scheme, W.J. Braithwaite, records in his autobiography how what might have then appeared as a short-term fix would have a devastating long-term political consequence.[11]

One danger which even Braithwaite did not notice followed from nationalising the work of friendly societies and mutual aid organisations. The government now had its national system—of sorts—and began taking a determined interest in the affairs of the member bodies, particularly their financial reserves. The reserves became a special target for governments, who cut the Exchequer's subsidies the more societies were successful.[12] And, as so often in these stories, irony was ever present. The crippling of the societies' reserves was turned around and used in a public campaign against mutuality. The critics of voluntary collective effort found it easy to point to the inadequate level of benefit payments, the different levels of benefit payments, as well as the groups who were still left without cover.

This was the political battering ram which was used to break down the defensive gates of mutuality. The charge that the system had failed immediately to provide cover for everyone in the land carried with it the capital sentence. Yet, ironically, a major responsibility for this very state of affairs rested with governments which, by raiding the reserves, crippled efforts to move towards a greater universalisation of provision.

Health Services

Now to the last of the three faces of welfare before the state
tightened its grip to the point of a near monopoly. The roots
of health services, like education and social security, cut
deep into our history. The hospital system was run by a
church which then carried out many of the functions of a
modern state. It ran the learning business, as it is sometimes so ineloquently billed today, and by its relief of
poverty it has the right to claim founder membership of our
social security system. Hospitals, in medieval times, were
not restricted to functions they carry out today. Shelter,
food, and rest, as well as long-term care, was what hospitals
then offered, in addition to nursing the sick. Hospitals, and
the foundations which supported them, ebbed and flowed as
population moved, as wealth-holdings changed, and as the
temper to establish such bodies similarly fluctuated over
time. In the Tudor era some of them, particularly but not
exclusively those in London, also carried out what today we
would see as a welfare to work strategy.[13]

Given that voluntary provision of hospitals was considered to be a legitimate part of the political scene up to a
little over 50 years ago, it is surprising how quickly the
extent of such provision has disappeared from the public
memory. By then, of course, voluntary hospitals were not
the only providers of care. Over the five decades prior to
their nationalisation, local authorities became increasingly
important suppliers in this area. One of the recommenda-
tions of the 1909 minority poor law report stemmed from
Beatrice Webb's insistence on breaking up the old system by
delegating many of the poor law functions to specialised
local authority departments. A poor law medical service was
on the march well before the 1909 Royal Commission
Report saw the ink at His Majesty's Stationery Office, and
it was a form of provision for which local authorities took
responsibility after the Neville Chamberlain reforms. It is
one of those interesting asides which tells us so much about
the motivation of some politicians, their ability to think long
term, as well as the changing pecking order of Whitehall
ministries in relation to the Treasury that, in 1924, Cham-

berlain refused to move back to No. 11 Downing Street and insisted instead on going to the Ministry of Health. He went to this department with plans for 25 bills, 21 of which he successfully enacted.[14] Chamberlain, as much as anybody, has a claim to be placed amongst the founders of today's welfare state.

A dual system of provision, by local authorities and voluntary bodies, was the pattern of the inter-war hospital service. It was these hospitals which constituted the putty from which Aneurin Bevan shaped the hospital (as opposed to the health) service we have today. The public opinion survey Beveridge commissioned on post-war reconstruction recalls the priority voters registered for a national health service. Beveridge, ever one to spot a winner, reported in a few rolling Bunyanesque paragraphs that one of the key aims of post-war reconstruction must be the establishment of a National Health Service. Satisfied, perhaps, that his claim to founder membership of the NHS was secure, Beveridge moved smartly on to consider the other assumptions on which his report was built.

Whether the establishment of the NHS is part of the consensus which enveloped not only the Churchill wartime coalition, but governments covering the following three decades, is now questioned in historical debate. What somewhat surprisingly commands so little attention is not only how the nationalisation of the hospitals was played between the two major parties, but how it was seen by the main government players, and particularly by the Prime Minister, his deputy Herbert Morrison, and the enigmatic Minister of Health, Aneurin Bevan.

At the outset, it has to be recorded that Labour ministers seem to have cared little for the voluntary status of the many hospitals which served their constituents. The duel, when it came, was between Herbert Morrison, the begetter of the LCC in its most powerful form, and Aneurin Bevan, the Tribunite left-wing firebrand. And the ground on which they crossed swords was over the fate of the local authority hospitals. There seemed little concern at all over the state acquisition of the voluntary hospital movement.

Who would run the hospitals, to whom they would be accountable, and how they would be financed, were not subjects which Attlee thought important enough to comment on in any of his writings after the collapse of the Labour government in 1951,[15] even though the NHS was seen as one of his government's greatest successes. Nor is there any mention of these questions in the official biography of Herbert Morrison,[16] despite the fact that it runs to over 650 pages and that here was an issue where Morrison is being proved to have had the better judgement.

Michael Foot's monumental life of Bevan proves the exception to the rule. Here the complexity and the range of issues involved are considered, perhaps understandably, as the NHS was such an important achievement for Bevan. But this outstanding study is partisan, and has the great strengths but also the weaknesses of such an approach. The author's socialism, like Bevan's, was one of state centralisation. The Bevan charge sheet has a familiar ring to it. Doctors were paid different amounts, hospitals begged for money, and hostility prevailed between those maintained by charitable bodies and local authorities. The great teaching hospitals stood aloof and, 'above all', no comprehensive arrangements for building hospitals where they were most needed had ever been contemplated.[17]

We ought now to be able to see clearly that nationalisation did not automatically cure any of these defects, and that each of these might have been tackled effectively by a radically different strategy. One of Bevan's principal charges was that the old system has not produced any new hospitals. Yet, if this was such a condemnation, what we are to make of the fact that the country had to wait until Enoch Powell was Minister of Health before a hospital building programme was announced, let alone enacted. Worse still, 'All the tenderness towards local vested interests (shown by the Coalition government's proposals) was abandoned', with Michael Foot adding 'Bevan had little patience with those who defended small hospitals on the grounds of intimacy and local patronism'.[18]

Similarly, short-sighted charges were commonly made about hospital funding. Voluntary hospitals, as opposed to those run by local authorities, were unable to raise all their costs. Again, the charge sheet emphasised that voluntary hospitals in London raised only a third of their expenditure and those in the provinces about a quarter.[19] These figures need repeating. What could a national health service do today with additional funds of this magnitude? These were sums raised in addition to the fees coming to the hospitals from the insurance cover derived from Lloyd George's 1911 Insurance Act.

So hospitals owned by local authorities, and those run by charities and voluntary bodies, were nationalised—the cleanest and most immediate death to be suffered by any part of the non-state welfare considered here. That nationalisation of welfare proved no panacea has become obvious to an ever-widening proportion of the electorate. Again, the life of welfare before the state took control offers direction and encouragement to today's reformers.

The Third Way

Since the 2001 General Election the debate on welfare has entered a new phase. Not only does blaming the Tories carry less and less credibility, but Labour's record on centrally run public services is under the voters' spotlight as never before.

History is likely to see the present government's attempt radically to improve public services as the last throw in the politics of central control. If a one-third real increase in monies going to the NHS does not begin to produce a noticeable improvement in services, for example, what will? That the Secretary of State for Health has to issue a central edict on how to clean hospitals suggests there is a paralysing weakness inherent in a centrally-run service which almost no amount of money will cure.

Failure of this centralising strategy does not automatically mean that common services must suffer the fate of privatisation, although that is undoubtedly what the Tories will offer. There is a genuine third way which was tried in this country at a time when voters rejected state control with as much vehemence as they resisted market direction.

Education, social security and health were once organised on a common basis outside the state's domain and safeguarded from the vulgarities of a free-market system. Very significant numbers of parents ran their own schools. Social security was organised on a common basis by means of mutual societies. Most of our health services were set up and financed by local effort.

The hour is late for those voters who wish to see education, social security and health delivered on a collective basis. But to ensure their long-term support the centre-left thinking has to move swiftly beyond a single model of centrally run services. The ration-book economy, for that is what centrally run services have to be, will become less and less palatable as voters see themselves primarily as consumers making choices about timing, quality and the means of delivery. The only way collective services can meet these criteria is for the consumers to run the provision themselves.

There are at least three political conclusions to draw from this essay. The first is the reassurance that comes from knowing that there was collective welfare before the state moved in to create a near monopoly supply. Only recently is it assumed that all forms of collective provision must be state-run. Second, there were forms of welfare which were consumer-led and operated. Huge advantages stem from this kind of ownership, both in the matching of benefits with real needs and the self-policing against abuse. Third, in respect to education, here was a service run by the least affluent group of the population. Support for non-state collective welfare has not historically been limited only to more affluent working-class and middle-class groups.

4

Lloyd George and Gordon Brown: How the Welfare Reform Titans Compare

Summary

Lloyd George and Gordon Brown are often compared as radical Chancellors of great talent and drive. There should be no question that both are political figures who have not only dominated their respective parties but who, as Chancellors, became the main players in their respective governments. But the strong similarities of these two substantial players conceals a major difference in their welfare strategies. Lloyd George sought not simply a reform programme to universalise existing provision. He possessed a clear view about how human nature operated and how to work with it in a way that added to the public good. In contrast Gordon Brown's welfare strategy looks only at the immediate impact of each measure and judges it solely on whether it increases the income of the recipient. Increasing the income of those on low income was only half of Lloyd George's agenda, and not the most important half. Increasing the income of the poor while simultaneously widening their freedom was the crucial goal of Lloyd George's welfare reforms. By contrast, Gordon Brown's reforms will create a serfdom whose income cannot be changed by their own efforts, but only on the say-so of politicians.

Gordon Brown and Lloyd George are sometimes compared in their roles as Chancellors of the Exchequer intent on reforming welfare. As I was perhaps amongst the first to make such a comparison, I would like to use this opportunity to develop the theme. There is much in common between these two major politicians. Both men have been significant forces in transforming the politics of their respective parties. Both have as Chancellors extended the remit of the Treasury across government, although even Lloyd George could be forgiven for any surprise he might feel about Gordon Brown's adventurousness on this front.

Both men see themselves as welfare reformers *par excellence*. And it is from an examination of their record on this issue that lessons can be learned for the new parliament. In two fundamental ways their approaches diverge. Their views about how revenue is best raised when taxpayers are less enthusiastic than they might be in meeting Treasury demands could not be more different. Their understanding of how human nature responds to the kind of welfare on offer shows a similar fundamental divergence of views. An examination of these differences constitutes the bulk of this chapter. But first, does the background of each of these major political figures help explain these fundamental differences which I believe separates them?

Class Background

Both Lloyd George and Gordon Brown have Celtic origins. Simply to mention their geographical roots highlights how open the British Establishment has proved to be over much of modern history. Just how open British society has been is illustrated if we take the century stretching from the conclusion of Victoria's reign to her great-great-grandchild's Golden Jubilee. That openness has extended not simply to the upwardly mobile working class go-getters born on English soil. Individuals from the constituent parts of the kingdom have been similarly advanced.[1] Not only are Celts, particularly those from north of the border, over-represented in the present Cabinet. The office of Prime Minister has similarly been more often occupied by candidates whose origins would have once been described as Northern Britain than the size of its population would justify. Both our principal characters share a common experience of being born outside the English metropolitan élite and of making their way via election to the United Kingdom parliament and then to national, and in Lloyd George's case, international political success.

The class origins of both of our principal characters do spell out a significant difference, however. Gordon Brown was born of the manse. Not rich by any stretch of the imagination, but it was a middle-class household living on a stable if modest income. Lloyd George's childhood circumstances mark him out from the cultural life which inevitably surrounds a middle-class family like the one in which Gordon Brown grew up. Lloyd George's father died before he was born. It was his mother's brother—Richard Lloyd—who responded to her pleas for help by taking the fatherless family into his own home.[2] The prospect of destitution was prevented by a strong family network—the first and safest of all welfare states. Yet this difference must be carefully qualified. Richard Lloyd's family was more highly cultured than are most middle-class families today. He not only employed labour, but had a knowledge and love of literature to an extent which leaves admirers of the national curriculum's achievements speechless. Lloyd George was not immune to this particular teacher's abilities and culture.

Yet the family backgrounds do spell out the first of the substantial differences between our two heroes which will play such an important part in explaining their widely different welfare reform strategies. Lloyd George confided to one of the people who accompanied him on his pre-World War One fact-finding tour of the German national insurance system that only those who had experienced it really knew what poverty was about. This is a difference to which I shall return.

Radical Difference

The radicalism of the two men also provides a point of contrast. Gordon Brown's parliamentary life has been one of blossoming under the shade of a friendly and protective parliamentary leadership. Lloyd George was a rebel whose rebellion helped propel him to a leadership position. The Welshman's rebelliousness was most apparent on two of the most divisive issues of late nineteenth-century and early twentieth-century British politics.

On the first, the Boer War, Lloyd George was not simply divided from the Liberal leadership, but from the bulk of the country as well. The fiery Welshman's anti-Boer War stance proved so provocative that on at least one occasion he was lucky to escape with his life from an anti-war public meeting. Here, in passing, we see another of Lloyd George's qualities on display. There was no compromise on the main issue at hand. But on a secondary and more immediate issue, how to escape from Birmingham Town Hall with body and soul intact, Lloyd George was more than willing to accept police advice and be smuggled away in a less than dignified manner.

Events have not conspired such that Gordon Brown has had to take a stand in war-time which separated him from mainstream opinion. If such events had offered that opportunity then possibly it would have happened over the Balkans conflict. His stance here was so mooted that I doubt if anyone could now state what Gordon's position was on this issue in the years up to 1997.

The second issue where Lloyd George's radicalism was shown was on his method of political opposition to the 1902 Education Act. A hundred years on, it is hard to visualise the fear and distrust then between church and chapel over many issues, and particularly on the operation and payment for elementary education. Over half of all elementary school children were educated in Church of England schools. In many areas the church school was the only one on offer. Non-conformist parents had no option but to send their children to the local Anglican school.

Many such parents objected strongly to being made to finance church schools which supported dogma about which they strongly disagreed. While extending secondary education, the 1902 Act also entrenched the Anglican position. It also requested non-conformist rate payers to help finance the reform.

After hearing the Prime Minister, Arthur Balfour, introduce the Bill, Lloyd George's immediate response was encouraging.[3] He then saw the non-conformist vote in

England move swiftly into opposition. The Boer War had divided the Liberal Party, with most of the coming politicians in the Liberal Imperialist camp and opposed to Lloyd George and his allies. The 1902 Education Act gave Lloyd George the chance not simply of restoring good relations across this party divide, but of leading the campaign. In doing so he encouraged a form of direct action amongst nonconformists over the non-payment of the education rate. The details do not concern us here. But Lloyd George's stance could not but have added stimulus to the growth and appeal of syndicalism and direct action which was to spread so rapidly in early twentieth-century Britain and which was to cause such problems for the Liberal government once elected in 1905.

Here then is another point of contrast. While Gordon Brown's radicalism was apparent during the earlier part of his parliamentary career, the direction of his radicalism is markedly different from that of Lloyd George. Gordon Brown's role was to challenge, along with a select few, Labour's socialist inheritance that had proved so electorally damaging. An analysis along the conventional left/right divide[4] suggests Gordon Brown helped to move his party to the centre. Lloyd George, in contrast, helped pull his party to the left, and in doing so proved to be a key figure in translating the new Liberalism into a legislative programme. He was also, over the Education Act, an advocate of non-Parliamentary opposition.

Taxing Differences

Fiscal policy is central to the role of the Chancellor of the Exchequer. On this front too a fundamental difference is apparent. Take the question of redistribution. Lloyd George made much of the redistributionary impact of his budgets and none more so than the one he delivered in 1909. Indeed, he appeared to go out of his way to rough up the opinions of those who would lose most under his Chancellorship. Gordon Brown, by contrast, believes that current politics demands that any redistribution is wrought as discreetly as possible.

Fiscal policy provides a further divide between our two powerful characters. Gordon Brown's Exchequer steward-ship has been in large part an exercise in strengthening the fiscal status quo. A policy began by his Labour predecessor, Denis Healey, was ruthlessly consolidated by a succession of Tory Chancellors. It has been a policy which proved exceptionally successful during the 1997-2001 parliament. This approach marks Gordon Brown out as one of the more successful of post-war Chancellors and the most successful ever of Labour politicians to hold the post.

In contrast, Lloyd George saw his role as a destroyer of financial orthodoxy. He broke the long-standing Gladston-ian budget consensus in a number of very significant respects. Colin Matthew has discerned the social contract of the Victorian state stemming from the balance struck between the incidence of direct and indirect taxation.[5] It was in Gladstone's 1853 budget that a financial contract between classes was laid down which was to last half a century. Gladstone's aim was for taxes on wealth, income and spending to be held in a balance that was perceived as fair across classes. In achieving this objective, two princ-iples became widely accepted.

First, the budget sought to raise revenue in a way which integrated the nation rather than exacerbated class divi-sions.[6] Under Lloyd George the budget ceased primarily to be an instrument of social integration, and it was from this angle that Lloyd George made his first attack on Glad-stone's budget orthodoxy.

Lloyd George also began to rewrite what had been the accepted balance between local and national taxation and in so doing gave rise to the second of his moves to create a fiscal consensus more to his own liking. As Chancellor, Lloyd George changed the balance between local and central collection of taxes on the one hand, and the balance between local and central spending of that revenue on the other. A century later we are now in a position to see the severe downside to each of these moves.

Springing Asquith's Tax Trap

Another major difference between Lloyd George and Gordon Brown arises over what constitutes taxation and how revenue can best be raised in an age of growing taxpayer resistance to the demands of the Exchequer. Asquith's 1908 Old Age Pension Act had been financed from direct taxation. An innovatory welfare reform measure had been conceived and gestated in the womb of budget secrecy. No discussion amongst Cabinet colleagues had taken place before Asquith made his views known to the House of Commons in his budget statement.[7] It took almost 20 years to free pensions policy from the restraints of financing pensions from direct taxation.[8]

Asquith believed that there was simply not sufficient revenue to pay other than a five-shillings-a-week means-tested pension. From this point reformers were dealt a near deadly hand. The pension was accepted as inadequate, but the Exchequer lacked the revenue to make it more generous. Additional revenue could only come now from direct contributions for the pension, but how was it possible to argue that people should pay into a pension scheme, or provide other savings themselves, which would give them an income only slightly, if at all, more generous?[9] The negative impact means-tested provision has on behaviour had now surfaced in the political debate and there it has remained ever since. But, it would appear, the lesson about the impact of means-testing on behaviour in the longer run has to be relearned by each generation.

Asquith's financial strategy for funding the old age pension, as it was then called, locked Lloyd George into a financial cul de sac on a second front. Pension reform fell from the political agenda and was not to resurface for a further decade and a half. But the financial block on major pensions reform pushed Lloyd George's mind into one of its many creative exercises. Not for the first or last time, welfare reformers looked to the continent for inspiration. Off went Lloyd George with his close circle of friends to examine what Bismarck had done 20 years previously.

Bismarck had faced a similar fiscal restraint to the one confronting Lloyd George. The federal government had not then been conceded tax-making powers by the German states so newly federated into a nation. National insurance was Bismarck's answer. Lloyd George could have hardly believed his luck. Here was a revenue-raising measure which was popular. It would, moreover, fit like a glove over Britain's political culture where friendly societies and mutual aid bodies had by means of collective but non-state insurance begun to transform the well-being of working people.

National Insurance Divide

It is on their attitudes to national insurance that the first of the significant welfare differences between Lloyd George and Gordon Brown lies. It also illustrates their fundamentally differing interpretations on what constitutes taxation, as well as their interpretation of voter attitudes to taxation.

When Lloyd George was Chancellor working-class people did not pay income tax. They did, however, pay indirect taxes and these payments were resented. Not an insignificant proportion of Gladstone's working-class support stemmed from the cuts he made in indirect taxation, paying for these reductions from the increased revenue the Exchequer had been accumulating from economic growth.

National insurance was in Lloyd George's hands to prove a means of financing the National Health Insurance Scheme, both sickness, disability and unemployment benefit, as well as the payment of free access to a doctor and free medicines. The concessions into which Lloyd George was forced by the powerful industrial insurance companies when he was attempting to fashion these national schemes are considered elsewhere.[10] The appeal national insurance contributions would have to a working-class electorate who, then as now, saw little virtue in paying taxes (as opposed to other people paying them on their behalf) was only too well appreciated by Lloyd George.

National insurance contributions universalised payments that had been regularly made by many working people to one or more of a whole range of friendly societies. These friendly society contributions were not seen as a tax. They were expenditure which people undertook freely. Moreover, to which friendly societies these payments were made depended on the choice of the consumer. Choosing which friendly society to join, and later, whether to move to another society, offered a degree of consumer choice unknown in a state-run service. The early views about national insurance payments as a continuation of friendly society contributions help to explain why national insurance contributions were so easily bedded down into a political culture. They were not seen as a tax. According to recent government research, this is a view still held by the overwhelming majority of contributors.[11]

Voter resistance to paying tax is not as recent a phenomenon as it is sometimes portrayed. Lloyd George was only too well aware of the restraint this placed on him when he began to think about the funding of his welfare reform programme. National insurance contributions were his way of squaring this fiscal circle. A rather different response to the appeal of national insurance is drawn from Gordon Brown. His attitude is far less favourable. The present Chancellor sees national insurance simply as a tax. That was the line he adopted in the television broadcast following his first budget. His actions on this front are surprising for a number of reasons.

In an age of growing voter resistance to tax levels, the Chancellor is not content with re-badging national insurance as a tax, despite all the evidence to the contrary of how voters perceive these payments. As if to ensure as far as any Chancellor can decide that insurance payments are considered as a tax, the Chancellor has also moved from the DSS into the Treasury the operation and collection of national insurance contributions, together with those civil servants concerned with developing national insurance policy.

Those actions of Gordon Brown leave a nagging question in the mind of the observer. Why, in an age when voter resistance to taxation grows, should a Chancellor re-badge national insurance as a tax when contributors hold stubbornly to an opposing attitude? If the welfare reform programme is about meeting new needs, as well as existing needs, and is not simply concerned with reining back on universal welfare expenditure, why would a welfare reforming Chancellor ignore this attraction of national insurance?[12] Lloyd George did not and was able thereby to extend the protection of welfare without a popular outcry about tax levels.

Defying Human Nature

This takes our discussion on to a second, linked issue. Do these two Chancellors agree on how welfare impacts on character? Is welfare an irrelevant consideration to how people behave, or can it help shape for good or ill how people go about their daily lives? Here both Chancellors share a common starting point. Both believe welfare affects behaviour. It is once we begin to consider the dynamics of that impact that a most fundamental difference between these two gifted characters once again emerges.

The key ingredient of Gordon Brown's welfare reform programme is the introduction of a whole series of what he calls tax credits. Here is not the place to consider whether the constituent parts are tax credits or whether a more apt description would be social security benefits masquerading under another name. The point at issue is the range, scope and conditions on which support is offered.

The tax credit flag ship is undoubtedly the working families tax credit (WFTC) which replaces the social security benefit family credit. Introduced in 1999, the WFTC currently pays on average £77 a week although, as we shall see, the average payment disguises just how large individual payments can be. Families with children earning below a prescribed level are eligible for a credit together with a significant additional credit towards the costs of childcare. Eligibility extends in some instances to beyond the income point at which the higher rate tax becomes payable.

There are other tax credits already in operation and the system is to be extended to single people without children in 2003. At this point the care component of the working families tax credit is to be hived off and combined with an integrated child tax credit. People without children may be eligible for what will then be called the employment tax credit. The complexity, not to say jumble, of differing tax credits has been wittily mocked by David Willetts.[13]

The point at issue for this discussion is the impact of tax credits on behaviour. In one sense the Chancellor sees tax credits as influencing behaviour for the good. The whole of his strategy emphasises that work pays and the mechanism to deliver this guarantee is the tax credit system. People are made better off, sometimes very substantially. But the impact of this strategy, sadly, is not thought through. What is offered is essentially a static analysis at the point at which a new welfare benefit is introduced.

What is most required is an account of how welfare shapes behaviour over a longer period. In the first year of tax credits the Chancellor's policy of making work pay is a clear success. But that is by no means the end of the story. What is of utmost importance is the cumulative impact over time of how tax credits influence how people work. Interviewed on the BBC's 6 o'clock TV news on the night of the 2001 Budget, a low-paid worker expressed thanks for the extra WFTC cash. He then added, unscripted and unprompted, that he realised that he would now never be able to improve his family's living standards by his own efforts. That would only come by politicians changing benefit rates.

The reason for this particular expression of anguish is that tax credits are means-tested. As a recipient's income or savings rise, the tax credit is reduced. Moreover the tax credit does not run in isolation from other means-tests. The WFTC acts as a passport to the two other important means-tested benefits, housing benefit and council tax benefit. The average value of these two benefits alone to working families currently stand at £55 for a two-parent and £59 for a single-parent family.

The cumulative withdrawal rate for these three means-tested benefits, together with tax and national insurance deductions, rises to 95p in the pound. Hence that strangled

cry of the low-paid worker interviewed on BBC News. Nor
will that worker be a lone voice. The Institute for Fiscal
Studies estimates that 83 per cent of families with children
are now eligible for the working families tax credit.[14] The
poverty trap has come of age.[15]

Working with the Grain of Human Nature

A fundamental assumption about how human beings
operate inevitably underlies the tax credit system. A
fundamental part of the pre-1997 Labour rethink was on
how welfare impacts on character. Tax credits fly in the face
of all the moral noises Labour made in the run up to that
crucial election that this most simple but crucial of assumptions would constitute the basis of Labour's welfare reform
programme.

Gordon Brown's right hand acts knowing that incentives
are important. But his left hand appears unaware of the
dependency he is creating directly from the particular kind
of incentives he offers. The Chancellor sees that people can
be motivated to work and to save, but he sees incentives as
though all that is required, and all they achieve, is to kick
start the human engine. Nothing could be further from the
truth. In welfare it is the long-term impact of policies which
is of key importance.

How does this view of the way welfare shapes behaviour,
both over the short- and longer-run, compare with the
assumptions about welfare and behaviour which underpinned Lloyd George's welfare reform strategy? None of the
rules in the 1911 Health Insurance Scheme for sickness or
disability benefits, or the payment of doctors' fees, discrimi-
nated against those who had savings. Eligibility was
determined solely on a person's contribution record. Working, saving and being honest were rewarded.

The assumptions underpinning Lloyd George's design of
the unemployment insurance system are equally important
to our current debate. The scheme was operated through
the trade unions—itself a characteristic action by Lloyd
George who would always use existing machinery wherever
possible. An old and trusted means of delivery maximised

the chances that the benefits would arrive in the right hands, in the right amount, on the right day.

Playing for safety was only part of the appeal to Lloyd George of a trade-union based welfare. He appreciated the importance of those working-class organisations which tried collectively to improve the living standards of their members. His reforms aimed at strengthening the position of trade unions. Indeed his hope was that 15 million members of the working classes would become organised as a result of the Act.[16]

The trades first covered by unemployment insurance were not simply those most prone to sharp periods of unemployment. No doubt partly because of their precarious nature, trade unions already provided some insurance cover in these trades to those members who quickly lost jobs as trading positions worsened. Here is the key to understanding how Lloyd George believed a state system could best work with the grain of human nature. Lloyd George's goal was to provide a universal benefit to those working in the defined trades so that it underpinned as opposed to neutering or destroying any voluntary effort.

Voluntary effort was welcomed and encouraged and was to provide additional provision on top of the state minimum. The mechanics to achieve this goal could not have been simpler. A weekly 7s benefit was paid out by trade unions for which the unions would be reimbursed for three-quarters of the cost, i.e. 5s 3d. If, however, the union persuaded members to insure themselves for at least an additional 2s 4d a week benefit, the trade union would regain from the insurance fund the whole of the 7s paid out on the state benefit[17] and the worker would gain a substantially higher income while unemployed.

Trade unions operating outside prescribed trades were in addition encouraged to set up their own unemployment insurance scheme for which they would receive one-sixth of the cost up to a maximum benefit of 12s a week. Members in these trade union schemes were not required to pay any contributions into the Insurance Fund, and the rebate, or 'bribe', as it has been called,[18] was paid from Treasury funds and not from the insurance contributions paid by other workers. It was by such a simple but ingenious method that Lloyd George built a floor below which no one could fall but on which every encouragement was given for individuals and groups to provide a more generous welfare cover.

Spinning Out of Control

This approach of Lloyd George to reform could not be more different to the approach Gordon Brown is following in his tax credit strategy. The immediate appeal of tax credits is one of concentrating help on households with the lowest income. Yet this immediate appeal will prove no more than a passing phenomenon once the impact the tax credit system will have on the behaviour of recipients becomes apparent.

The initial skirmishes between tax credits and human nature will not be immediately apparent. Indeed, the first signs of that struggle, shown in a rapidly rising tax credit bill, will be spun as the clearest possible sign of the success of the strategy. More and more money, it will be claimed, is going into the pockets of the poor. Who could object to such an outcome?

The second phase of the tax credit debate has already dawned. Claimants are already working the system and so are employers. There are reports of some WFTC recipients gaining a job and registering their children at a nursery and, knowing that any working and childcare credit runs automatically for six months, withdrawing their child from nursery and ceasing to work themselves. The tax credit payment—which for a single parent on the minimum wage and gaining a net pay of £106.22 a week is £348.45 per week —then runs until the end of the six-month claim period. The same process of gaining a job and a nursery place, and then ceasing to work and withdrawing the child or children from the nursery at which they are registered, will begin all over again. And who can blame claimants for working the rules in this way? No job offers such a reward, and when an income from tax credits can be three times the original income, who can blame claimants who settle simply to live on the tax credits?

Let me illustrate the scale of tax credit generosity. A single mother, for example, earning £4.10 an hour over a 30 hour week will see her net weekly income of £106.22 more than quadruple to £447.34 once the child care tax credit and the basic working families tax credit are added in. A yearly net income of £5,523.44 once the tax credits are added in is equivalent to an annual salary of £23,261.68. Even more staggering is the level of earnings a single mother would have to achieve to give her an income equal to, let alone a penny more, than her current entitlement. Gross earnings in excess of £31,500 a year are now required to put the person on an income equal to an individual earning £4.10 an hour and claiming all the tax credit help available.

This is just one example of how generous the Chancellor has made his tax credit scheme and how attractive the credits must be to recipients. But tax credits are like a wasp trap. For the trap to work the jam has to be intoxicating. And, like a wasp trap, once a person is into the tax credit system, few will be able by their own efforts to escape. More importantly, the system's generosity will bring forth a new industry whose purpose is simply to work the system to the full. In no way could any other action by individuals—apart from winning the Lottery—make such a difference to their standard of living. Working the system will be a major consequence of introducing tax credits at such a generous level.

Tax Credit Fraud

The system will also be open to straightforward fraud. The rewards tax credit offers are too great for this not to be so. Many inspectors of firms where employees were gaining the family credit (the precursor of working families tax credit) reported the very significant weekly cash sums taken from the bank about which employers became totally vague when questioned by the inspectors as to the money's destination. These were firms where workers were generally on wages which afforded them the highest family credit payments, and the suggestion must be that in addition to the FC payments and wage packets workers were picking up cash-in-hand. The same fate awaits any Speenhamland-type subsidy to low wages.

Then, once corruption enters into the system, as it inevitably will, and where a growing body of claimants and employers work the system to their full advantage, a steep change will take place in the debate. Panic will grip the public imagination. Stories of fraud will become a more regular feature as an ever escalating tax credit bill is reported.

One clearly unintended result of the working families tax credit and its offspring will be to push low wages down towards the minimum level. That trend will be exacerbated as soon as the employment credit covering single people and childless couples comes into play. Collusion will be one force that will work here, with workers and employers cheating taxpayers by registering low wage levels which are false. But other employers will rightly begin to question the sense of raising real wages when such a strategy does not increase the family income of their lowest paid employees. From that point onwards employers paying wages towards the bottom end of the income scale will see the best policy as one of holding wage levels (and indeed reducing them for new recruits) and encouraging employees to maximise their income through WFTC and the employment credit. It will not be long before entrepreneurs have produced software for employers to work out how best to maximise through the tax credit system the take-home pay of each and every one of their employees.

For anyone doubting this outcome, I ask them to recall all the glamorous razzmatazz which surrounded the advent of housing benefit. Then, as now with WFTC, the birth of housing benefit was greeted with almost universal approval. The government was seen to be helping the poor pay their rent. And, again, who could possibly be against such a laudable aim?

That particular welfare reform then begins to develop under the momentum which is inherent in any means-tested welfare scheme. A diet of escalating rents, rising corruption and housing benefit bills out of control, left the government with little idea of how to control the monster it had created.

WFTC will be a re-run along the housing benefit trajectory except that this time far greater sums will be involved and, unlike housing benefit, whose birth had all party support, the tax credit system will be seen to have a clear political parenthood. Stories of fraud will become a more regular feature as an ever-escalating tax credit bill is reported and, under the media pressure, the government's nerve will crack. It will begin the search for a painless exit strategy. No such exit will be found no matter how diligent the search.

A New Serfdom

These two political Titans already have very different welfare reform records. Observers will naturally speculate on the extent to which the different upbringings of these Chancellors help to explain their widely different approach to welfare reform. Lloyd George reported his personal knowledge about poverty set him apart from other reformers who lacked this experience.

Whatever the reasons, it is the different understanding the two Chancellors have on the role of human nature working with or destroying welfare reform that separates these two major figures. Gordon Brown has, no doubt for the very best reasons, unwittingly launched a tax credit welfare reform programme which will ensnare most working people. A new serfdom is being created. A government which gained in 1997 an outstanding election victory partly on the basis of its determination to destroy welfare dependency is ending up by extending that dependency beyond what anyone could have seriously imagined.

And it is a form of permanent serfdom that is being created. There is now no way by which those most dependant on tax credit will be able by their own efforts to free themselves from this welfare dependency. Worst still, the standard of living this dependency offers will ensure a working of the system on an unimaginable scale. It will also, because of the huge sums involved, open up a totally new gold mine for fraudsters. From now on the government, not individuals by their own effort, will decide the living standards of the vast majority of working families with children. To rip out the mainspring of a free society—the drive to improve one's own lot and that of one's family—as WFTC does, cannot but harbinger ill for our country.

Compare this with Lloyd George's approach. Each of his reforms—establishing a national network of labour exchanges, the beginnings of unemployment insurance, a national system of health insurance for working men and women—worked with the grain of human nature. Lloyd George's strategy was to build a minimum floor to underpin a growing proportion of the working population. On that floor Lloyd George was careful to ensure that individuals could then by their own efforts substantially improve their standard of living.

Gordon Brown's tax credit strategy is similar to Lloyd George's approach only in the sense that he too is anxious to increase very substantially the incomes of the poor. But the means he has chosen do not underpin individual effort by building an income floor. The opposite has occurred. Tax credit builds a ceiling which is now so thick that only a minority of claimants will ever be able to free themselves from this form of welfare dependency.

Both of these Titans have as Chancellor of the Exchequer been concerned about increasing the income of the poor. But it is only Lloyd George who has with equal skill and determination ensured that increasing the income of the poor was only half of the agenda. Lloyd George had two objectives he simultaneously set about achieving. The first was to increase the incomes of those at the bottom of the pile. But setting them free as independent and full citizens was of equal or of greater importance. The widening of freedom, while simultaneously increasing the income of the poor, is not an objective which can be achieved from a tax credit reform.

Conclusion

In one sense Gordon Brown has been by far the most adventuresome of the two welfare reforming chancellors considered here. Not only has much of the machinery for running welfare been transferred to the Treasury, but the aims of welfare policy have been transformed. Instead of acting as a compensation for the costs of human and market failure, Gordon Brown now sees welfare for those of working age bound up with his attempts to raise the long-term growth rate of the British economy. While Lloyd George's initiatives were highly original, and cut new ground, they in no way challenge Gordon Brown's ambition. But Lloyd George's strategy was one which understood how human nature worked, how it responded to financial and welfare incentives, and how human nature's reactions to these stimuli had to be fashioned to the public good. Gordon Brown is creating a degree and intensity of dependency for the working population hitherto unknown. In stark contrast Lloyd George's welfare reforms were all concerned with building floors under the poorest so that they could rise by their own efforts. Gordon Brown's strategy of simply raising the income of the poor was only half of Lloyd George's agenda. Widening their freedom was his ultimate goal.

5

Offering a New Tax Contract:
Public Choice in the
Age of Low Taxation

Summary

The reported death of the electorate's wish for low taxation is, to adapt a phrase by Mark Twain, much exaggerated. At what level taxes should be pitched remains a central political question. Yet talk of a single response to the level of taxation puts the matter too simply. Financing long-term increases in health and education and general expenditure needs to be viewed differently, as does a policy towards the rest of public expenditure. Health offers the chance to develop a national insurance-based scheme of finance which could provide the basis for a buoyant means of financing the NHS. Education advance calls for a different approach where a genuine third way between mega private school fees and parent fund-raising activities can be developed. It is on the basis of the differing appeal of the main areas of public expenditure that the government would be wise to reshape its long-term tax policy.

The Political Culture of High Taxation

First then, what do the polls tell us? They appear to present a fairly uniform message. Voters are recorded as being against the modest tax cut which came into operation in April 2000. Taxpayers would like to see more spent on health, and, the politicians allege, on education as well.

Lecture arranged by the Haberdashers' Company, St Lawrence Jewry, London, 23 March 2000.

These findings need to be handled carefully. Britain is still the inheritor of a political culture set down by the Attlee government. A determination not to go back to the 1930s was understandable, and the atmosphere that the war left was conducive to the post-war venture. We had all been part of winning the victory. A similar collective endeavour was called for in winning the peace, as it became known.

That the country was bankrupt was a factor hidden by the fact of being one of the three victorious powers. If the political governing class realised this crucial fact, it behaved as though the idea was foreign to it.

The massively high taxation of the war years slid easily into the norm for peacetime activity. Top rates of 83 per cent on earned income and 98 per cent on investment income were at first a necessity to help pay for the reconstruction—along with American loans and Marshall Aid, of course.

That the pay of working people had been pulled into direct taxation as a result of war financing appeared not to register with politicians. Taxation, in contrast to a century earlier, came to be seen as a moral goal in itself, as distinct from what the resulting revenue was used to achieve.

The Left became hooked. In an age of growing uncertainty in beliefs here was a new yardstick to help judge good and bad, right and wrong. Whether one was or was not in favour of high taxation became an ever more important touchstone for those on the Left who were anxious to disengage from the 1940s definition of socialism. In this new, uncertain world, high taxation was seen not only as a good, but as a crucial distinguishing mark. It became a proud badge for the Left to wear.

How much this enthusiasm was shared amongst the electorate can be doubted. A detailed breakdown of the electorate's response cannot now be constructed. But there are events which suggest that this high taxation appeal did not carry all before it. Whenever the chance presented itself, the electorate broke from Mr Attlee's ration-book model of the good life.

The 1950 election result is every bit as important as that of 1945 when gauging the meaning of the post-war political arithmetic. The Tory opposition appeal was limited. After the 1945 landslide, who could blame them for lacking too much political nerve? Yet Labour's 146 majority almost disappeared in one go. Eighteen months later Labour's brave new world was over. It is a truism, worth remembering today, that what the electorate gives it is capable of taking away.

The Tory appeal gained confidence. 'Trust the people' rang in harmony with voters, even if Tory politicians remained nervous about taking their own rhetoric too seriously. Lower taxes played a part in each of the Tory election wins of the 1950s. Despite every help they gave to the Opposition's campaign, the Conservatives almost won in 1964.

In addition to 1950, there were two more decisive post-war elections. Fighting in 1979 was a weird experience. For Labour there was not only the shame associated with the winter of discontent. The shift in the vote was summed up by the comment Jim Callaghan made to Bernard Donoghue as they motored back to Downing Street after an election meeting, that a sea-change in voters' perceptions was taking place. Labour's hold over its vote was fracturing. After a longish period of two-party government offering near comprehensive public services, sometimes of dubious quality, voters pushed the balance once again towards what they thought would be lower taxation and greater choice.

1997 is the other crucial election result. Labour was again returned to power after an 18-year exile. But the political barriers to Downing Street were only removed on the understanding that Labour was now a low-tax party. In particular, the promise was not to raise direct taxation. Without Tony Blair's appeal, combined with this commitment, I still do not believe Labour would have won that election.

So here, then, is part of the tension underlying much of today's politics. For five decades the electorate has been bombarded with centre-left talk of the moral worth of high taxation. No wonder therefore that voters register to pollsters their willingness to pay higher taxes. To do otherwise in the current climate is to appear to the interviewer base, greedy, or even vulgar. But in practically every election over the past half century, when a clear choice has been presented on the taxation issue, voters have voted for a low-tax party. Of course, other factors have been relevant to the outcome of these elections.

Here is just one of today's many political paradoxes. Part of *New* Labour's appeal is its commitment on direct taxation. But that has long been the electorate's settled position, a position which has become more not less marked over the past half century. What is new is Labour catching up with many of its own supporters. Putting up other people's taxes to pay for public services had a certain political appeal. Pushing up one's own tax bill for services over which one had all too little command has a lot less political mileage.

The Primacy of Health's Appeal

Where does this view on voters' reluctance to raise direct taxes leave health and education funding? I do not believe that major, continuous improvements in both of these public services can or will be paid for by general increases in taxation. I do believe that these two key public services will require a scale of financing in the longer term over and above the rich pickings fiscal drag currently offers.

Health and education do, however, have their own special appeal to taxpayers. The attraction to voters of the first is more general, the second is more specific.

For reasons I still do not fully understand, the NHS has an appeal to voters which leaves all other public services trailing in its wake. In war-defeated Europe, social security, particularly pensions, commanded this position. Given the miserable, not to say miserly, sums paid to pensioners in pre-war Britain, any of us would have been awarded good marks for prophesying in 1945 a similar settlement for Britain. Yet, while pensions are a clear, outward, visible sign of the new post-war settlement in mainland Europe, the NHS took that lead role in Britain. Propose a relative cut in public pensions and mainland Europe comes out on to the streets. Offer to reform the NHS here and voters, at best, view the prospect with a caution, sometimes bordering on hostility.

Sixty per cent of NHS expenditure is on staff costs. Wages rise faster than prices. Drug costs also rise faster than do prices generally. Hence health costs invariably rise well above the general rate of inflation. Health costs are greater for the very young and for the elderly. An ageing population therefore adds to the pace of the rise in health costs. And to these factors we can add what appears to be an exponential growth in the costs of the ever-expanding market of health technology.

The willingness of voters to add substantially to the NHS budget should not be read across to all areas of government activity. And the extra money to pay for health needs to be ring-fenced if voters' support is to be maintained over the longer-term.

This discriminating stance of the electorate suggests that one way to advance would be to build the national insurance health contribution into a new, dynamic means of long-term health finance. I have detailed this reform elsewhere.[1] The suggestion is:

- in the first place, to finance the Prime Minister's commitment to raise NHS expenditure to the European average in six years by building on the health component of the employee's national insurance contribution

- and secondly, progressively to expand this contribution to cover the existing NHS expenditure.

The NHS would continue to be free at the point of use. The NHS would gain a buoyant source of revenue. The electorate would gain a specific means of financing health which established a direct relationship between payment of funds and their use. The fund would be ring-fenced from the sticky fingers of politicians. A health insurance scheme would free the funds currently allocated from general taxation for tax cuts.

The 2000 Budget saw the Chancellor responding to the hallowed status of the NHS in British political culture. The aim of the immediate increase of £2 bn for the financial year 2001-02, and the further increases in subsequent years, is for voters to see an improved service. This should be welcomed by all shades of the political spectrum. Nevertheless the extra cash will not achieve the Prime Minister's target of bringing Britain's health expenditure up to the EU average. And, because the plan is a long-term one, financed out of general taxation, the vicissitudes of the economy may undermine the commitment. A national insurance base for health would separate public funds that voters want to be spent on the NHS from other uses. Surpluses built up in good years would not be spent on other services; rather they would be spent during lean years. NHS funding would be assured even when economic conditions enforced spending restrictions elsewhere.

An Educational Opportunity

Education presents a different prospect. Both health and education have large private sectors. But the purchasing of private education is a much more determined business, lasting sometimes continuously for 13 years.

Part of today's social division in education results from the efforts of those reformers whose goal has been ostensibly to lessen the social divide. The closure of grammar schools has done more for the growth and sustaining of private education than any other act.

It is again one of those 'rich' ironies of British politics that on the record alone Mrs Thatcher stands as the patron saint of those reformers intent on closing the remaining 157 grammar schools. She, after all, sanctioned the closure of more grammar schools than did any other Minister of Education. Mrs T makes Anthony Crossland, Labour's Education Secretary who elevated destroying grammar schools into an article of socialist faith, a mere whinger by comparison.

The anti-grammar school campaigners picked what was to be their first victim with care. Because of its geographic circumstances, the number of signatures required in Ripon for the ballot was relatively small. The campaigners' judgement could not have been more misplaced. The easy prey turned out to be anything but that. Parents voted decisively to keep the grammar school.

Those of us in favour of keeping the existing grammar schools should not rest on our laurels. The campaigners for the destruction of grammar schools will only be defeated if the grammar school debate is set in a different context to the one it now occupies. The specialist and academic schools can only look forward to a secure future once all schools become specialist schools.

Both parties have made hesitant steps in this direction. I was reminded recently by the father of the city technology college movement that, when the Tories heralded the first ten such colleges, I criticised the initiative as being too timid and hoped that the approach would deliver 1,000 CTCs. The 500th CTC has since been announced.

In the wake of the Ripon vote, David Blunkett, as Secretary of State for Education, announced the establishment of Academies. But these schools will only operate on the site of failing or failed schools. One way of preventing Academies from being stigmatised in the way I fear they will be under the present proposals would be to offer Academy status to all non-CTC schools.

Each Academy, achieving well over the whole curriculum, would be expected to develop at least one specialism for which the school excelled locally. These centres of excellence—in languages, IT, sport, science, music, and maths— would choose their intake, and would have their intake decided for them by parents and pupils on the basis of matching a pupil's potential and known abilities to the school's specialism. All schools would become selective for the first time ever.

It is within this framework that it might be possible to raise more successfully income directly from parents. The present régime offers a growing proportion of parents the choice of private schooling, at fees of thousands of pounds. At the other extreme, in the state sector, contributions to school budgets are made through parents' association fundraising activities. A genuine third way to help increases in the education budget is urgently required.

A successful state school which provided the specialism most needed for an offspring could become a serious competitor to a private school option. In these circumstances the question becomes by what mechanism might parents who currently pay tens of thousands of pounds in school fees contribute to the budget of a specialist state school to which they decided to send their children?

The school which some of the children of the Prime Minister and his wife attend, the Brompton Oratory, provides the most likely way forward. Every school parent is expected to covenant part of their income for the time their children are at school. The contributions are linked to ability to pay.

The Brompton Oratory approach would need to be balanced by other changes if this move were to become a genuine third way approach to financing schools. Taxpayers making covenanted contributions to their children's specialist school would need to be content with the fairness of this overall approach. The existing core budgets would remain and would grow, as the country became richer. The budget would, however, need to be attuned so that those schools with the poorest parents would gain larger shares of public expenditure. But because the education budget from taxpayers would continue to grow, all school budgets would increase in money terms.

Here I believe is the genesis of an idea which could run. But if the Brompton Oratory approach is not to disintegrate, and is to play a part which reinforces rather than abates the social division of English education, it needs to be universalised and linked to the other educational reforms I have briefly outlined here.

Conclusion

There are risks with any strategy. Singling out those parts of the government's budget which have greatest support from taxpayers, and devising ways by which significant increases in the budget can be delivered on these fronts, may expose the least popular parts of government expenditure to attack. But I have assumed that over the next couple of decades resistance to tax will grow. Striking up a new partnership with voters in the way I have suggested will hopefully achieve two objectives. First, it will see an expansion of health and education provision. By the success of this strategy, of taxpayers feeling they are rightly seen by politicians to be in the driving seat, the second objective will hopefully be achieved. Politicians will gain a better hearing when defending the other areas of the government's budget. Of course here, and in health and education, the taxpayers will expect a rapid transformation in the delivery of these services. That is, I am sure you will agree, a topic for another time and another place.

Notes

2: Welfare and Citizenship

1 Churchill, W.S., 'The untrodden field of politics', *The Nation*, 7 March 1908.

2 Some working-class men gained the vote in 1867 and others in 1884. But the main bulk of unskilled working men did not gain the franchise until 1918 when the size of the electorate increased threefold: up from 7.5 million to over 21 million voters. Women did worse. Although they won the vote for elections for poor law guardians, women did not gain a parliamentary vote until 1918 and even then only on their 30th birthday. Age equality for voting was only established in the lifetime of my parents—in 1928—and single voting only in my lifetime—in 1948.

3 See Pugh, M., *The Making of Modern British Politics*, Blackwell, 1993, for an excellent introduction on how contemporary participants saw politics operating around the time of the Second Reform Act.

4 Abram, M., Rose, R. and Hinden, R., *Must Labour Lose?*, London: Penguin, 1960.

5 The proposal is presented in detail in the report of the Pensions Reform Group, *Universal Protected Pensions: Modernising Pensions for the Millennium*, London: Institute of Community Studies, 2001. This report is now being followed up with working parties looking at key aspects of the proposals.

6 This was the line argued in the welfare reform Green Paper, entitled significantly *New Ambitions for Our Country: A New Contract for Welfare*, Cm 3805, London: Stationery Office, March 1998.

7 Harris, J., 'Political thought and the welfare state 1870-1940', *Past and Present*, 135, May 1992.

8 The claim is even more impressive than this. The spending plans to 2001/2 project an average increase of 0.2 per cent each year (excluding tax credit) or 1.1 per cent (including tax credits). This lower rate of growth is largely attributable to a real terms fall in benefit expenditure in each of 1997/98 and 1998/99. Growth in each of the three subsequent years, i.e. after 2002, is

expected to be well above that in each of the last three years of the Conservative government.

9 *New Labour: Because Britain Deserves Better*, 1997, Manifesto, 25.

10 See Harris, J., 'Contract and Citizenship,' in Selsdon, A. and Marquand, D., *The Ideas that Shaped Post-War Britain*, London: Fontana, 1996, p. 137.

3: New Third Way Politics

1 Harris, J., 'Political thought and the welfare state 1870-1940', *Past and Present*, 135, May 1992.

2 I cite myself as a 'good' example here. I had to build up my own reading lists from footnotes of works I had come across. It was only after completing this section that I was introduced to Eddie West's fine work on private schools, West, E.G., *Education and the State*, London: IEA, 1970.

3 West, *Education and the State*, 1970.

4 Finlayson, G., *Citizen, State and Social Welfare in Britain 1830-1990*, Oxford, 1994, p. 1. Emphasis added.

5 Gardner, P., *The Lost Elementary Schools of Victorian England*, London: Croom Helm, 1984.

6 Sutherland, G., *Policy-Making in Elementary Education 1870-1895*, London: OUP, 1973.

7 Simon, B., *Education and the Labour Movement, 1870-1920*, London: Lawrence and Wishart, 1974.

8 Thane, P., 'The working class and state welfare in Britain, 1880-1914', *The Historical Journal*, Vol. 27, No. 4, 1984.

9 Quoted in Gordon, P., 'Lord Sandon and the centenary of compulsory education', *History of Education Society Bulletin*, No. 18, 1976.

10 MacBriar, A.M., *An Edwardian Mixed Doubles: The Bosanquets versus the Webbs: A Study in British Social Policy, 1890-1929*, Oxford: Clarendon Press, 1987.

11 'Being the Memoirs of W.J. Braithwaite', Bunbury, H.N. (ed.), *Lloyd George's Ambulance Wagon*, Cedric Chivers, 1970, p. 212.

12 Whiteside, N., 'Private agencies for public purposes', *Journal of Social Policy*, 12, 2, 1983.

13 Leonard, E.M., *The Early History of English Poor Law Relief*, reprinted London: Frank Cass, 1965.

14 Ramsden, J., *The Age of Balfour and Baldwin, 1902-40*, London: Longman, 1978, p. 27.

15 Attlee, C.R., *As It Happened*, London: Odhams Press; Clem Attlee The Granada Historical Records Interview, Panther Record, 1967; and Williams, F., *A Prime Minister Remembers*, London: Heinemann, 1961.

16 Donoghue, B. and Jones, G.W., *Herbert Morrison*, London: Weidenfeld and Nicholson, 1973.

17 Foot, M., *Aneurin Bevan, 1945-60*, London: Davis-Poynter, 1973, pp. 106-07.

18 Foot, *Aneurin Bevan, 1945-60*, p. 132.

19 PEP, *Report on the British Health Services*, 1937.

4: Lloyd George and Gordon Brown

1 If one part of the United Kingdom has a right to register a complaint it should surely be Northern Ireland, although the unwillingness of its citizens to come to London so as to attempt an assault of the greasy pole says much for their common-sense.

2 Lloyd George, as his biographer reminds us, was a privileged child, born not to rank or riches, but to a special historical opportunity. Grigg, J., *The Young Lloyd George*, London: Eyre Methuen, 1973, p. 17.

3 Again it is John Grigg's biography to which readers are referred. This is a classic study which relates the principle subject to the times in which he lived. It also, on numerous issues, provides the surest guide to the importance of individual events. His study of the 1902 Act, like so many events covered in the volume, is a classic miniature portrait shedding much light on the surrounding people and events while holding Lloyd George in central focus. See *Lloyd George: The People's Champion 1902-11*, London: Eyre Methuen, 1978, chapter 2.

4   This conventional analysis suggests to be left in Labour Party politics requires promotion of greater nationalisation along the Attlee model. Radicalism for the Liberal Party one hundred years or so ago was bound up with the new Liberal programme of greater state involvement and regulation. The limitations of such a categorisation of Labour's left/right axis only has to be expressed to be seen. Yet such a categorisation is used in the media to sound notes of approval or disapproval.

5   Cited in Jenkins, T.A., *The Liberal Ascendancy, 1830-1866*, London: Macmillan, 1994, p. 112.

6   By decreasing the size of the national debt Gladstone appealed to the working class who saw the City through higher interest rates as the main beneficiary of government borrowing. Retrenchment also struck a blow against the army and placemen who cornered the market in public pensions, and who were thus seen also as another of the main beneficiaries of the Exchequer. Daunton, M.J., 'Payment and participation: welfare and state-formation in Britain 1900-1951', *Past and Present*, 150, February 1996, p. 173.

7   Walley, Sir John, *Social Security: Another British Failure*, London: Charles Knight, 1972, pp. 30-32.

8   It took the genius of Neville Chamberlain, a much underrated welfare reformer, to break through the political cul de sac into which Asquith had driven pensions reform.

9   The Unionists, as the Conservatives were then generally known, had the answer. Their key amendment was to exclude the first £40 p.a. of friendly society income from the income calculations for the pensioners. Typically Bentley B. Gilbert, whose whole tract has the theme tune of welfare rightly moving towards stage monopoly provision, dismisses this move as the Unionists' 'chief attempt to wreck' the scheme. Gilbert, B.B., *Evolution of National Insurance in Great Britain*, London: Michael Joseph, 1976, p. 223.

10 I recall this and other events in a forthcoming paper on welfare reform and civil society.

11 Davies, R., Hill, M. and Williams, T., *Attitudes to the Welfare State and the Response to Reform*, Research Report 88, Department of Social Security, Analytical Services Division, 1999.

12 Sense is made of the Chancellor's obsession with calling national insurance a tax if stage two of the tax credit strategy is to rein back national insurance, push more people on to means-tested tax credits, and reduce tax by slashing what were once called national insurance contributions.

13 Willetts, D., *Browned Off: What's Wrong with Gordon Brown's Social Policy*, London: Politea, 2000.

14 Brewer, M., Clark, T. and Myek, M., *Credit Where It's Due? An Assessment of the New Tax Credits*, London: Institute for Fiscal Studies, 2001.

15 Field, F. and Piachaud, D., 'The poverty trap', *New Statesman*, 1971. This is the first time this phrase was used.

16 Grigg, *Lloyd George: The People's Champion 1902-1911*, 1978, pp. 337-38.

17 Gilbert, *Evolution of National Insurance in Great Britain*, 1976, p. 279.

18 Gilbert, *Evolution of National Insurance in Great Britain*, 1976, p. 280.

5: Offering a New Tax Contract

1 Field, F., *How To Pay For the Future: Building a Stakeholders' Welfare*, London: Institute of Community Studies, 1996.

Independence: The Institute for the Study of Civil Society (CIVITAS) is a registered educational charity (No. 1085494) and a company limited by guarantee (No. 04023541). CIVITAS is financed from a variety of private sources to avoid over-reliance on any single or small group of donors.

All publications are independently refereed. All the Institute's publications seek to further its objective of promoting the advancement of learning. The views expressed are those of the authors, not of the Institute.